For the mist people, for the fish people,
for the wave people and the rock people.
For the madrone and the fern people.
For the cloud and the wind people,
for the gull people and the crow people,
the grass and the buttercup people, for
the clod people, the worm people, the
beetle and the fly people. For the
slug and the duck, the sheep
people and the goat people. The cabbage
and the rose people. For the mouse
and the house people.

All my relations, all my relations.

Winter
Gardening
in the Maritime Northwest

Cool Season Crops for
the Year-Round Gardener
2nd Ed.

Binda Colebrook

Maritime Publications
Everson
Washington

Maritime Publications
P.O. Box 527
Everson, WA 98247

Cover Design, Elizabeth Watson

Illustrations:

Robert Williamson; Savoy Cabbage on cover and pages 24, 25, 26, 32, 38, 52, 67, 68, 80, 91, 93, 97, 100, 104, 105, 107, 111, 113, 114, 116, 120, 121, 125, 126, 131, 135, 136, 142.

Carol Oberton; pages 5, 8, 9, 10, 11, 45, 46, 47, 58, 60, 72, 109, 152.

Rebecca Samson; dedication page and pages 12, 46, 48, 89, 98.

Gerrit Byeman & Associates; pages 61, 70, 76.

Bob Benson; map on page 8.

Peter Warshall, page 7. Reprinted with permission from *Shelter*, 1973, Shelter Publications, Bolinas, California.

Jody Aliesan; "Waiting," page 31, reprinted with permission from *Soul Claiming*, 1974, Mulch Press, Northampton, Mass.

Shunryu Suzuki, pages 40 and 77, reprinted with permission from *Zen Mind, Beginner's Mind*, 1970, John Weatherhill, Inc. New York, NY.

David A. Stone, page 35. Reprinted with permission from *Know and Grow Vegetables 2*, by P. J. Salter and J. K. A. Bleasdale, 1982, Oxford University Press, Oxford, England.

Dr. Leanne Hinton, page 52. From "For the Land Knows You're There," 1982, reprinted by permission from *Tying a Knot in the Devil's Tail*, Larry Hanks, Bellingham, WA.

M. Nieuwhof, page 90. Reprinted with permission from *Cole Crops*, 1969, CRC Press, Inc., Boca Raton, Florida.

David MacKenzie, pages 150-151. Reprinted with permission from *Goat Husbandry*, 1956, Faber and Faber, London, England.

Library of Congress Catalog Card Number 84-60085
ISBN 0-916239-00-4

Copies of this book may be ordered from the publisher at list price. Washington residents add 7.5% tax. Inquire for quantity discounts.

ACKNOWLEDGMENTS

Writing this second edition, was for me, a much harder job than the first, and I certainly hope you all think it's been worth it. I do! In spite of the time it took this edition is clearer, more accurate, and has a lot more information for the aspiring winter cropper.

Many thanks are due. To Jim Rosenau, for starting the ball rolling, and to Marsha Morrison and Dan Levant for keeping it going.

To everyone, too numerous to name, who has written to me, filled out feedback forms, answered my many questions, sent me information from research stations both here and overseas, and in general aided the cause of winter cropping. To all those seed companies who sent samples and answered questions, but especially to Johnny's Selected Seeds, Abundant Life, and Territorial for their work in introducing the proper varieties for northern and maritime climates of the United States.

Great thanks are due to my patient and tactful editor and friend Lane Morgan, who has helped this second edition to be a lot easier for you to read, and to my partner at Cloud Mountain, Tom Thornton, who carried most of the mental and physical burden of the farm work while I fiddled with words and reconstructed paragraphs. Also to Dennis Scott of Nooksack Tilth, and Craig MacConnell, Whatcom County Extension Horticuluralist, for giving constructive criticism to the manuscript, and to Marlene Maskornick and Dale Johnson for proofreading it.

Mark Musick of regional Tilth, and Mike Maki and Pat Labine of Evergreen State College's Organic Farm Program all gave substantial help with the production process. Mary Ballard of Just Your Type was her usual competent self *and* remarkably tolerant of my numerous changes. Bill Sodt and Dave Porter of Fairhaven Communications gave advice along the way as well as flying through a complicated pasteup job.

Blessings on you all!

Cloud Mt. Farm
January 1982-1984

The writing of this second edition was made possible in part by a grant from the A. B. and Flavia McEachran Foundation through the good offices of Marshal Morrison, and by an anonymous grant.

TABLE OF CONTENTS

What This Book Is About

I wrote this book for people living in the maritime Northwest who would like to have more fresh vegetables in their gardens during the winter months. It will be especially useful to people who have learned their gardening in a continental climate, who are not aware of the possibilities of a maritime climate, and hence, close up their gardens from October till May.

It will also be useful to people who have grown up in and gardened in this mild environment without being aware of the many winter varieties and good seed sources available to them.

This book is about those vegetables and their varieties that regularly come a crop between October and May. These are often termed cool season or cool weather crops. They are not *sown* in the winter, but *harvested* then. While some sowings can be done as early as February and March or as late as October, most are done from April through September.

If you think about this for a bit, you will see that growing winter crops means that you turn from a summer gardener into a *year-round gardener* (a lot more work by the way!). I suppose I really should have written a book about year-round gardening, but if I had done that, I would have had to devote space to tomatoes and cucumbers when it is the cool season crops that need to be discussed. Also, you might have missed the point: the point is that in this climate you don't have to be without vegetables in the fall, winter, and early spring if you use the right varieties, observe the right sowing dates, understand the principles of cool season production, and experiment for yourself!

The Principles
of
Winter Gardening

Climate

mama earth

The earth turns eastward round her poles. Our main wind comes to us from the west, across hours of ocean, damp and restless. That mass of ocean air gives us our climate, known as maritime, from the coast to the Cascade Mountains. This climate is just what is needed for winter gardens in the higher latitudes. It exists naturally along *west* coasts, peninsulas and islands from about 37 to 59 degrees latitude, give or take a bit due to ocean currents and other factors. If you look at a world map, you will see that parts of Europe, Japan, Tasmania, the south island of New Zealand, and Chile are all within this range. In North America the area from northern California to northern Vancouver Island in British Columbia, and parts of the Alexander Archipelego are also suitable. Further north, although the coastal climate is mild, there is little arable land, and high precipitation and lack of winter daylight prevent most winter crop production.

A maritime climate is distinguished by its cool, even, humid nature, both summer and winter. Here on the west coast of North America temperatures hang around 40 °F in the winter with occasional changes in either direction. Spring and fall are long, slow affairs—misty, cloudy, and rainy—trying to the patience of the human inhabitants.

For vegetables, however, this murky weather is easier to deal with than the sharp, dry cold and sudden temperature changes of a continental climate. In fact, *many* of our common vegetables are well adapted to it. The long falls that gradually turn colder give vegetables ample time to prepare for winter, to "harden up." When the first frosts come, they are usually accompanied by high soil moisture and high air humidity. The latent heat in this water vapor is returned to the air as the water condenses in the form of frost, preventing sudden drops in temperatures. The misty mornings are another plus as they give frozen plants plenty of time to thaw out gradually before they are touched by the sun. (Later, in the long, cool springs, plants can produce lots of growth before bolting with warm weather and longer days.)

Winter does come, though! Around the time of the winter solstice, the dry, cold air masses east of the protecting mountains tend to flow over and bring a week or two of continental-type weather to us. Snow, though hard on traffic, is a blessing to the garden as it protects the soil and plants from freezing, insulating them in a snug white blanket. It is when cold comes *without* precipitation and the soil freezes deeply for long periods of time, and when dry winds blow, that you can expect to lose many of your winter vegetables.

The winter of 1978-1979 was like that in Washington, with frigid weather from Thanksgiving until February. But still, in my garden in Whatcom County near the Canadian border, leeks, kale, parsnips, and carrots under their mulch, supplied winter food. And in March the unprotected spinach and corn salad, along with the lettuces under the cold frames, all revived, grew, and produced an abundance of salads. Sometimes these cold years run in bunches, as they did in the 1950s. It's hard to tell when they will come, but you can count on at least one year in ten not being very good for winter crops. Every twenty-five years or so the maritime Northwest gets a really rough winter like 1978-1979. However, even these aren't as bad as an average continental winter.

Different parts of the Northwest have variations on the general maritime theme. The whole coastal strip is milder and very rainy and windy. All the foothills are colder in winter with shorter and often cooler growing seasons. The inland valleys of southern Washington and the Willamette Valley in Oregon have slightly warmer summers and colder winters, while the Puget Sound region is generally mild. The northern islands suffer less rain but more wind and cooler summers. Wherever you live, in order to be successful with winter crops you must pay attention to your particular local climate. By experimenting you can discover which winter varieties are suited to your garden and what is the proper time to sow and transplant them.

> *Knowing that nothing, not even the Earth you are standing on, is standing still, is part of the Earth-shelter-yoga. The more you feel these vibrations (the whole biosphere breathing as a lung and exchanging energy like the breath), the greater joy this more accurate and truthful Energy Earth will bring.*
>
> *So find happiness in the fog, in mud, and dust. This is a plea not to indulge in criticism of the weather. As seashores sluff away and deserts turn to meadows, we are being entertained by the three states of matter that were the conditions for our life.*
>
> *Peter Warshall*

On a rare day of partial clearing clouds separate to reveal the Maritime Northwest. On the east, the Cascade Range protects it from the thirsty Plateau. On the west is the Pacific.

Southward the Siskiyous and Trinity Alps palisade the Maritime Northwest against the bare brown hills and burning plains of California. Northward, though maritime climate persists, agriculture ceases, turned back by mountains that rise from the surf.

CAPE MENDOCINO
Eureka
Crescent City
CAPE BLANCO
SHASTA
Klamath
Medford
Grant's Pass
Rogue
Roseburg
Umpqua
Coos Bay
SISTERS
Willamette
Eugene
Corvallis
JEFFERSON
Salem
HOOD
Columbia
Portland
Astoria
ADAMS
ST. HELENS
Cowlitz
Longview
RAINIER
Olympia
Tacoma
Puget Sound
Seattle
Aberdeen
Everett
Hood Canal
GLACIER PK.
Mt. Vernon
OLYMPICS
Skagit
Bellingham
BAKER
Strait of Juan de Fuca
CAPE FLATTERY
Fraser
Victoria
Vancouver
Strait of Georgia
VANCOUVER ISLAND
Nootka Sound
CAPE COOK
Queen Charlotte Strait
CAPE SCOTT

R. BENSON

Site

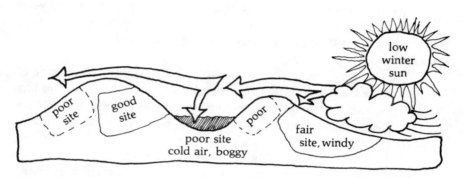

The best site for fall and winter crops is a gentle slope on the south side of a hill or a building. It might be a site you could terrace, with wind protection close enough to make a difference but not so close it blocks the sun.

A building reflects and holds heat; the slope aids in drainage; terraces make a warm microclimate; and wind protection allows that pocket of warm air to stay where it has developed.

Usually the best place for winter crops is also a good sun-bathing spot, so let that be your guide. When the sun comes out for a week during one of those January-February high pressure systems, you should be able to work comfortably in a shirt in the perfect site. I did in my garden in Seattle though just around the north corner of the garage it was still winter. That extra warmth means extra growth on your lettuce, corn salad, Brussels sprouts, etc., and hence, healthier plants and more food. It also means warmer temperatures at night and can make the difference between losing your plants to freezes or not.

Many a less-than-ideal spot, however, has produced an abundance of winter vegetables. If your choices for a garden don't include a particularly sunny spot (at least half a day of sun in the summer growing season), then you may have to limit the kinds of vegetables you will grow. Better to have lots of spinach, lettuce and corn salad, than Brussels sprouts and cabbages that didn't make it, especially if you are more likely to eat the former raw and hence, maximize your nutrition.

If your only sunny spot faces onto a street, beware. Traffic exhaust will be coating your plants, soil, and what's worse, your lungs, with lead, asbestos, and other nasties. My best advice is to move, but if you can't, be sure to wash your food well and not to garden during rush hour.

The warmest spot in fall and winter is usually the south side of a house, a traditional site of the perennial flower beds. If you like flowers, that's a hard thing to give up. Maybe you can fit lettuce and onion greens in amongst the asters. Be careful though: many garden flowers and bulbs are poisonous, and you wouldn't want to eat a daffodil bulb thinking it was an onion.

Drainage of both water and air is another very important aspect of a site. Low spots are poor for winter gardens. They collect cold air (hence early frosts) as well as water. A wet soil will be too cold for good growth and it will suffocate your plants. They need air around their roots. If you have water drainage problems in the middle of an otherwise desirable spot, it is worth the trouble to install tile, dig a diverting ditch, or make raised beds.

You can also have air drainage problems in the middle of a slope if you have barriers to the free flow of air. A tight fence *downhill* of your garden will catch the freezing air instead of let-

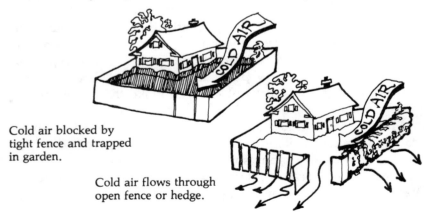

Cold air blocked by
tight fence and trapped
in garden.

Cold air flows through
open fence or hedge.

ting it pass on by. Use an open fence or hedge instead. However, a solid barrier *uphill* is all to the good as it deflects cold air and drying winds from the garden.

No matter how good a site you have in other respects, if the wind can blow away the warm air that has been built up, it won't do the plants much good. Plants are quite vulnerable to wind damage in the winter. For one thing, they become brittle and desiccated in freezing weather, and for another, when the ground is soft from lots of rain, their roots can easily be dislodged.

There are two distances at which wind protection is useful: 1) relatively far distances, fifty feet or more; tall structures like houses, barns, or trees fit in here; and 2) distances closer than forty feet which includes everything from a garden fence or hedge to shingles or cloches. With everything except transparent cloches you should make sure that your wind protection doesn't block the low winter sun.

If you have the space I think it's worth your while to make a walled garden out of whatever material you can scrounge. If you can control the design of your house and out-buildings you would do well to study European and New England farms, which are often built in a complex that leaves sheltered spaces. In the New England countryside the house and barns were usually connected, but

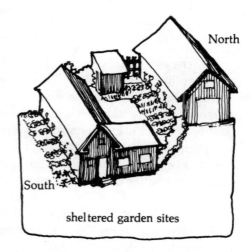

North

South

sheltered garden sites

that is a fire hazard and should be avoided. Hedges or fences connecting buildings would serve just as well. In the city or suburbs this protection happens automatically from the smallness of lots and the proximity of buildings.

If you want to make a windbreak for your garden or grounds

you have to decide what form to use. Although expensive, a fence is quick to build and is good if you have limited space. A hedge is slower (maybe five years), and you have to keep it pruned well at first to encourage density. It also uses a lot of space.

Sheltered area resulting from solid barrier equals
8 times the height of the barrier.

Sheltered area resulting from a 40% permeable
barrier equals 16 times the height of the barrier.

Whichever you choose, fence or hedge, a forty percent permeability is preferred.[1] This is because solid barriers, as the picture shows, shelter less distance to leeward and increase turbulence. A fence can be slatted and hedging material chosen that isn't too dense. Deciduous shrubs tend to be dense in summer and too permeable in the winter (with the exception of hedging beech, which keeps its leaves until spring), so one of the evergreens might be a better choice for your main planting. With the wealth of plant material available you can choose varieties that will grow to the height and thickness you desire. You can also consider including plants that are edible or medicinal, either for you or your livestock (see Winter Crops for Livestock).

Usually, wherever you live, there is a place you can find which will serve or a structure you can build or grow to help break the wind.

1. Pollard, et al. Hedges, pp. 164-5.

Soil

A great deal can be said about the nature of soil in relation to vegetable gardening. For the purposes of this book I will restrict myself to what is relevant to cold, hardy crops. If you want more general information, look in Books You Should Read in the Appendix. Several of them have excellent discussions of the nature of soil and its improvement or maintenance in the garden.

To begin with if you want decent winter crops, you must follow the same procedures of good soil care that you would use for decent summer crops. Only more so! This is because winter is a time of greater stress for most plants. Also, soil that is to overwinter crops must be well drained. You can't expect much good of your kale or spring cabbage, and especially your parsnips, if they have been standing in sog for a month. However, poor drainage is usually not an insoluble problem. Depending on the reason for it, drainage pipe, subsoiling, growing deep rooting green manures, building raised beds, and even moving your garden are all alternatives.

Soil type also affects cool season crops considerably. Light soils with plenty of sand warm up soon and drain well. They are good for late winter sowings and early spring crops. However, because they are less moisture retentive and less stable to temperature changes, they do not grow as fine nor as hardy a fall and mid-winter crop.[1] This is especially true for members of the brassica family, which are in the main such heavy feeders. A silt or clay loam, on the other hand, will be more complicated to improve, trickier to work, and later to warm up; however, such a soil can hold more moisture and nutrients and, hence grow excellent late crops.

The chances are that you don't have much choice about your garden's soil type and will have to make do with amending it to make it more suitable. Probably the single most important thing you can do as a year-round gardener is to focus on adding organic matter, especially in the form of compost and green manure residues.[2] This increases the *humus* content which aids in balancing the soil, making the whole gardening process easier and more fruitful. In terms of cool season production, humus has several roles. It aids in aeration. It acts as a buffer of pH. It allows for a slower, longer-lasting release of nutrients. During the cold seasons the presence of humus aids in holding a more even soil temperature so that plant roots do not suffer such extremes.[3]

Some of the best ways of adding humus to your soil are by green manuring, fallowing, adding manure or vegetable composts, and mulching.

There are many different methods of composting, and as almost every organic gardening book will tell you how, I am spared that task. It's an important practice, and no doubt you will work out a method that suits you.

Green manuring is a very useful, if not essential, component of soil care for year-round gardening in a maritime climate, and you would do well to include it in your gardening routine. Our high rainfall and frequent cloud cover guarantee a leached soil, which means an acid soil, with minerals and other nutrients being carried down into the subsoil by the rain. However, these nutrients can be kept in the topsoil by root activity, which also enhances soil life and helps control erosion. Overwintering vegetables and green manures both do this. Green manures are crops which are grown in parts of the garden or fields for a period of time and are worked directly into the soil just before the space is needed. A green manure can grow in the soil for as long as a year. At this point it is really a form of fallowing, but the purpose and end result are similar. Most often in our area, green manures are used on a more temporary basis if they are used at all.

Suitable green manures include grasses, rye and oats, buckwheat, mustards, herbs and legumes. Rye is typically used by farmers in this area for a winter cover crop; it is easily available and cheap. Its one great advantage is its ability to germinate and grow in low temperatures. You can sow it after your late harvests. However, its vigor is such that it is hard to kill in the spring. If it is a wet year and you cannot work your ground enough to kill the rye you often end up with it intercropped with your spinach and peas. Oats are an alternative to rye. In northern areas some varieties of oats winter kill, but they continue to hold the soil. Though they must be sown early in the fall, they are good for those beds that will have the earliest spring sowings. Summer vetch *(Vicia sativa)*, Phacelia, radish and pod peas are also good late catch crops that will usually winter kill in the North.

If you have trouble finding or can't afford to buy organic sources of nitrogen, legumes, in a mix or alone, are a preferred green manure. Fava beans, winter or hairy vetch *(Vicia villosa)*, wild lupines, Austrian field peas and crimson clover are good ones.[4] Except for the lupines, they are all easier to remove in the early spring than rye, and they leave varying amounts of nitrogen, as well as root residues, in the soil. These roots play an important part in making the soil friable and suitable for the next crops.

Green manures also suppress the growth of winter weeds. They can be undersown in vegetables in the late summer or early fall. My few experiments with this technique have shown it to be less practical for me than mulching.

Another important use for green manures is on empty beds that are waiting for summer sown winter crops. If you have such a bed bare for more than three weeks at mid-summer, it will substantially aid the following crop to sow it to buckwheat. A bed that is bare for a little longer can have a clover added in. This will discourage weeds, keep the soil from drying out, and add some organic matter and nitrogen when the green manure is worked or tilled in a few days before transplanting.

If your garden is large enough, and especially if you have problems with a hard pan, a heavy clay soil, or an excessively light, sandy one, fallowing is a good practice. This consists of taking part of your garden—a seventh is often recommended—and sowing it to green manure crops for the full year. The deep rooting biennials such as chicory or the legumes such as sweet or Persian clover and alfalfa are particularly useful. Buckwheat and Phacelia (Bee's Friend) are good annuals to put in the mix to bloom the first year. Rye grass is good for bulk in the topsoil.

Fallowed sections or beds should be mowed occasionally and the cuttings either composted or left to decompose on the soil.[5] This way minerals that are brought up from the subsoil by the roots of the plants are available in the topsoil for the vegetables you grow the following year. The roots also open up passages in the subsoil, helping to aerate it, and add organic matter as they decay.

Fallowing, like green manuring, makes use of the fact that different species of plants utilize and concentrate different nutrients, grow at different levels, have different diseases and pests, and respond to different seasons in their growth patterns. For the price of the seed, or less if you save your own, you can have a host of green friends working for you in your garden. This makes your garden somewhat more like a natural ecosystem. You are encouraging biological processes and de-emphasizing industrial and mechanical ones.

Where you have not had a chance to grow a green manure a simple hay mulch will at least protect the soil and leave it in a better condition for spring sowing. Mulching is an excellent way of increasing organic matter if used with discretion. I try to mulch those overwintering crops that stay in the open till April or May. This helps protect their roots and stems during freezing weather and encourages biological activity in the surface soil. It also suppresses weeds from late February through April, a time of active weed growth. True, mulch harbors slugs, but with the bigger winter plants I don't find the damage to be as much of a problem as weedy spots in the spring.

Clearly you want to choose your mulches to suit the crop. Leeks need a finer mulch than kale or cabbages. I don't mulch any spring or early summer sowings; in the wet, cool maritime climate the soil needs to warm up and lose some moisture. (This is less true of sandy soils than of silt and clay.) Nor do I mulch under frames or under crops such as corn salad that cover the ground well by the end of October.

Soil *color* also affects crops grown in the cool seasons. The darker a soil is, the better it absorbs heat. This heat is then radiated back out at night, ameliorating the temperature swings around crops grown in the surface soil. For this reason English gardeners used soot from their stoves as a fine mulch around early crops. Adding organic matter also darkens the soil, yet another reason for using it.

Correct fertilization procedures are good for any garden, but a proper balance of the major nutrients—nitrogen, phosphorus, and potassium (N, P and K)—is particularly important to cold season crops.[6] Gardeners tend to concern themselves most with nitrogen, but phosphorus and potassium materially aid in bringing a plant to maturity and hardening it for the winter, so these three must be in balance without an excess of nitrogen. Thus avoid gardening advice such as, "Well, Swiss chard and spinach are leafy greens, and therefore you should give them high nitrogen fertilizers to stimulate leaf production in the late summer and fall." The fast, sappy growth produced by such nitrogen is just what you don't want for hardy crops. The first deep frost will lay them back. Though you might not get quite the *fall* production out of a plant that is grown with balanced nitrogen, you will get more winter and early spring production because your plants will *survive* the winter. When the weather begins to warm up in late February or early March, then you can think of side dressing with a nitrogenous material, or foliar feeding with fish emulsion or the like to produce a flush of growth. If you need it, that is.

My soil is not particularly high in nitrogen, but my overwintering spinach and lettuce put on as much growth as I can keep up with in the spring. The fall-sown spinach bolts much later than the spring sown crop also. I suspect that this is because they have had all winter to develop a marvelous root system that the early spring-sown spinach cannot equal. I find they taste better too: a meaty, dark green, sweet quality that I don't find in the others.

Other elements may aid in helping plants to develop hardiness: calcium and silicon, for example, and perhaps some of the micronutrients and growth hormones in seaweed. However, the literature on the subject is controversial.[7]

Another traditional way to add organic matter to your garden is by using animal manures. These are best composted before going on the garden with limited amounts of dry carbonaceous materials such as hay, straw, or wood products such as wood shavings and sawdust. Hay and straw are more typically used in the continental climates and Europe. Most gardening and farming books are written from these areas and assume that animals are bedded in these materials. Such barn cleanings compost quickly and completely in four to six months, or at most a year. However, on the West Coast, due to the availability of wood by-products, most farms use wood products to bed their animals. Wood products are high in carbon and lignin and generally need three to four times the amounts of nitrogen and time to decompose than do hay and straw.

Often the percentage of sawdust to manure in barn cleanings is such that the nitrogen in the manure is used up in the process of partially decomposing the sawdust. This is, of course, even more true if the cleanings have sat around in the rain for a while as the nitrogen will most likely have been leached out. If this mixture is put on the garden, the decomposing bacteria will draw nitrogen from the soil to finish the job. This process may tie up the nitrogen for as long as a year.[9]

This doesn't mean that you should avoid manure mixed with wood products, only that you should make an effort to add supplemental nitrogen and allow longer times for composting. It is somewhat hard to suggest just how much nitrogen you should add. Most recommendations suggest three-and-a-half pounds of actual nitrogen per cubic yard of *raw* sawdust.[10] With barn cleanings you should need less. But, really, the only way to tell is to watch the action of the compost pile. If it does not heat up and the wood particles do not break down, you will need to add nitrogen. If, after the pile has cooled off and the worms begin to enter, you still find *lots* of wood particles you may be able to finish the process by adding more nitrogenous materials. If at the end of a year you still find a few particles, don't worry. At that point they will break down very slowly and will not tie up much nitrogen. These particles will also serve to aerate and loosen the soil; this aeration is helpful if you are working with clay and compacted silts.

If you are bedding your own animals and can control the process, well and good. Straw is the preferred bedding. If this is unavailable or expensive, hardwood sawdust is the next best. Alder, maple and birch are common local trees, or you might find such hardwood sawdust as oak or other imported woods at a furniture manufacturer. If you get your sawdust from a local mill, choose a time when they are cutting the hardwoods, the true firs, spruce, or hemlock. All of these rot fairly quickly. (For this reason, of course, they need higher *initial* amounts of nitrogen in the process.) Way down on the list is Douglas fir, and last of all comes cedar, which is very slow to break down and toxic to seedlings in its fresh state.[11]

Some small animals, such as rabbits, are kept without bedding. Their manure can be composted easily with vegetables and garden refuse. Poultry manure, especially chicken, is very high in available nitrogen and will compost hardwood shavings fairly quickly if mixed with other wastes. If pig manure is used it *must* be composted at high heat to kill parasites.

If you are near a dairy farmer who uses a solids separator—not common, unfortunately—try to obtain the solids left after the liquids have been spread. This material usually has no bedding and is still high in nitrogen. It will compost to a usable product within six months to a year. It is rather like a silage product, and like silage, can be used directly as a mulch. Silage itself is also an excellent material for the compost pile.

Behold this compost! behold it well!
Perhaps every mite has once form'd part of a sick person—yet behold!
The grass of spring covers the prairies,
The bean bursts noiselessly through the mould in the garden,
The delicate spear of the onion pierces upward,
The apple-buds cluster together on the apple-branches,
The resurrection of the wheat appears with pale visage out of its
  graves, . . .

Walt Whitman

1. Nieuwhof. *Cole Crops.* p. 26.
2. Up to 40% of *worked* volume of the soil is considered adequate.
   C. Mac Connell, Cooperative Extension Horticulture Agent, personal communication.
3. R. Otto. Carolina Center for Biological Husbandry. Personal communication. Incidentally, humus is the end product of decomposition, whether from your compost pile or in the natural environment. If you want to know more about its biochemical properties, read p. 274 of Wolf Storl's book, *Culture and Horticulture* (see References in the Organic section).
4. It is sometimes difficult to find seeds of green manure species. The following seed companies have carried them: Abundant Life, Chase, Johnny's Selected Seeds, and Territorial. Also try your local feed and seed stores.
5. Early spring and late summer seem best for sowing falloing crops to avoid competition with vigorous summer weeds. But you will have to work out sowing times based on your site and garden schedule.
6. Lists of materials high in the macronutrients can be found in the *Rodale Encyclopedia of Organic Gardening.* Many of the green manure crops are good phosphorus accumulators: lupine, sweet clover, buckwheat, turnips and mustard. If you feel you need a better understanding of the role of NPK in plant nutrition, read the relevant sections in Jerry Belanger's *Soil Fertility* (see References in Organic section).
7. Stephenson. *Seaweed in Agriculture and Horticulture,* chapters 11 and 12. H. Koepf et al. *Bio-Dynamic Agriculture.* p. 184, 135f.
8. Darrell Turner. Extension soil scientist and agronomist, retired; WSU Research Station: Puyallup. Personal communication.
9. Dried manure bought by the sack in Washington State, however, is required by law to state its NPK ratio.
10. Washington State Cooperative Extension. *Soil Management in Yards and Gardens.* EM 3000, p. 4.
11. A. C. Bunt. *Modern Potting Composts.* p. 31-35.
    Darrell Turner. Personal communication. I was not able to find anywhere a definitive list of the breakdown rates and resultant pH, etc., of common West Coast trees. If you have one let me know!

Soil References
Green Manuring: Principles and Practice. Otto Schmid and Ruedi Kaly. 1981. Institute of Biological Husbandry, Observil, Switzerland. Available from Woods End Agriculture Institute, Orchard Hill Rd., ME 04984. $4.00. Very interesting discussion of the qualities of many green manure species as used in Switzerland.
Guidelines for Manure Application in the Pacific Northwest. Cooperative Extension; Washington State University. EM 4009. Feb. 1976.

Organic

I myself grow organically. I get pretty good winter crops that way. I do this partly out of a peasant thrift and stubbornness (I have all this cow manure available!), partly out of regard for the obvious facts of the ecosystem, and partly out of a dislike of chemicals and poisons. I enjoy the processes of nature far more than I do the workings of the industrial age. That is, I think it's more fun, more interesting, and less polluting to see if clovers, for instance, can manufacture the extra nitrogen we need in our gardens.

It's not my place here to proselytize biological agriculture (which is a term I prefer to "organic") versus chemical or synthetic. It is, however, the way I am learning to garden and farm, so when I give suggestions in this book, they are mostly of that sort.

You *can* grow winter vegetables using chemical fertilizers and pesticides. It's done on a commercial scale, and I've heard from a few gardeners who do so. Nieuwhof, for instance, notes in *Cole Crops* that a combination of organic manure (stable, green, or compost) and chemical nitrogens often give the best winter cabbage crops. He doesn't define "best," so one doesn't know whether taste, nutrition, cold hardiness, and storage life are included along with size and yield.

If you are currently satisfied with whatever way you are growing, well and good. Your winter vegetables will probably be no less satisfactory than your summer ones. But if you want to read more about various biological approaches to food production, I have included a bibliography at the end of this section. I should say right away that there is easily as much hype and shortsightedness within the organic movement as there is within the chemical mainstream system. *You* have to practice and read with discrimination!

Organic References
How to Grow More Vegetables. John Jeavons. New edition, 1979. Ecology Action, 2225 El Camino Real, Palo Alto, CA 94306. Devoted to the "biodynamic French intensive" method of raised bed gardening. Needs adapting to fit maritime Northwest conditions.

Maine Organic Farmer and Gardener. A well written, informative monthly tabloid. Box 2176, Augusta, Maine 04330.

The Organic Gardener. Catharine Osgood Foster. 1972. Vintage Books. New York. Written by a Vermont gardener. The first half has a pretty good exposition of plant physiology and the kind of thinking and practice that goes into organics. The section on how to grow individual plants is strictly East Coast.

Organic Gardening. L. D. Hills. 1981. Penguin Books, 625 Madison Avenue, New York, NY 10022. This, like all of Hills' books, is very worth reading, quite modern with a minimum of organic "romance" and a maximum of experience. Available from Richters Herb Seed Catalogue (see Seed Companies).

The Organic Method Primer. Rateaver & Rateaver. 1973. Pauma Valley, CA 92061. A compilation of different views and practices of organic methods from the U.S. and Europe. A rather uncohesive book, but it does introduce you to a great many ideas.

Soil Fertility. J. D. Belanger. 1977. Countryside Publications. Waterloo, WI 53594. A very good introductory book to soil fertility from the organic point of view. Some overview of European methods, and basic practical outlook. A good place to start.

Bio-Dynamic Books
Bio-dynamics is one form of organic agriculture and perhaps the most "holistically" oriented. Certainly it's the most outspokenly "spiritual." Many of the books are written by native German speakers or translated from the German and are confusing for this reason alone. Still, many insights and gems are to be found and they are interesting reading, at least parts of them, for the devoted gardener or homesteader. Many gardening authors ignore their work; others, such as John Seymour (a member of the Soil Association, England's oldest organic group) makes scathing remarks! There is definitely a large factor in the bio-dynamic procedures of what Mike Maki (a Southwest Chapter Tilth member) calls the Cosmic Placebo Effect!

Culture and Horticulture: A Philosophy of Gardening. Wolf D. Storl. 1979. Bio-dynamic Literature, Wyoming, RI 02898. $9.50. Written in the Rogue Valley of Oregon, this is the most modern of the "BD" books. Interesting history of the organic movement in general and the BD one in particular. A pretty out front discussion of their concepts of cosmology.

Bio-Dynamic Agriculture. H. H. Koepf, B. D. Petterson and W. Shaumann. 1976. Anthroposphic Press, distributed by Bio-Dynamic Literature. Box 253, Wyoming, RI 02898. A very lengthy book and not always easy to understand. Worth having for the serious horticulturalist as an additional reference and counteractive to chemical methods.

Varieties and Saving Seed

The very best microclimate, and perfect site and soil, will still not produce many winter meals if you grow summer varieties for winter cropping. Summer varieties are bred for quick production, not for staying power. Winter varieties on the other hand, grow slowly (some are in the ground ten months or longer), have higher dry matter content, and are ready late in the fall, winter, or earliest spring.

Winter varieties are also usually much hardier than their summer equivalents. The tendency to slow growth and hence high dry matter content (which is also associated with higher nutrients) is partly responsible here. Curly Green kale is a good example of that: tough as nails but very nutritious. Broccoli is another good example. Italian Green Sprouting, DeCicco, and Waltham are common open pollinated varieties for summer and fall cropping. By making a later sowing than usual—July or August—some small winter heads can be obtained. I used to do that in Seattle. But when I started gardening in the foothills out by Arlington I found they were only hardy to about 15°F. This, of course, restricts their deep winter use to mild areas. The purple sprouting broccolis, on the other hand, will survive down to 5°F, which means they can be overwintered through a considerably wider range. Of course, some of that hardiness is due to their immature state as they go into the winter; they don't attempt to form the delicate flower heads until the worst of the weather is over.

One last example. Take leeks. These are the quintessential winter vegetable, and yet, there are varieties of leeks bred for the fall which disintegrate with a few frosts. They are super tall with long white shafts and pale green, thin leaves. Your true winter troopers are short, stubby, dark green, thick leaved (again with a high dry matter content), and take the worst of weather. Even if damaged at the core by prolonged deep frosts and desiccating wind, they will grow new centers and by late March be harvestable again.

Unfortunately, these winter-bred varieties are not all that easy to find. You usually can't just buy them from the seed racks at the local garden store even in the maritime Northwest. Most of the vegetable breeders in the United States are busy developing varieties that will all be harvested before the dry, cold arctic air masses sweep down over field and garden. The vast majority of the seed sales in this country are for such continental gardens; there is little point in large U.S. distributors carrying special winter bred varieties for the relatively small population of gardeners who would know how to grow them. Because of this, most winter gardeners order their seed from a few small northern based U.S. and Canadian companies that carry locally adapted varieties. They also occasionally order from English, European, and Japanese companies where such varieties are bred (see Seed Companies).

Once you get a hold of a few of these catalogs, how do you know which winter cabbage, leek, or cauliflower to choose for *your* garden? Since every garden and taste is different, a neighbor's or a seed company's recommended variety may not be the best one for you. And that goes for my recommendations, too. Till now I have liked Carentan leek, but you may try it along with Winter Mammoth and Alaska and come to prefer Alaska. In fact, in two years I might come to prefer Alaska. So the best way

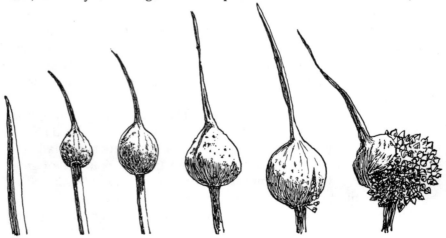

is to try out different varieties, but in a methodical manner. If you grow three varieties and one of them strikes you as pretty close to your ideal winter leek, then grow that for several years. This will give you a good idea of its abilities in different seasons and different parts of your garden. Then when you want to try new varieties, you have your "favorite" as a standard. Always grow the new and the old together, giving them the same sowing dates and cultural practices (fertilizing, transplanting, watering, etc.). Do this for several years. Observe the plants at as many different points in their life cycle as you can and keep good records. You will learn much more that way.

Once you have settled on the varieties you like, you may want to save your own seed. It's extra work and takes some planning and care, plus a personal vision of what the perfect parsnip (or carrot or kale) is within any given variety. But I think in the long run it's worth it. For one thing, you can no longer count on seed companies carrying old, tried-and-true, regionally-adapted favorites. The rush for new and better (usually hybrids) is well under way, and probably 75 percent of the old varieties have been lost or retired to the National Seed Bank and are no longer commercially available. Just as bad, the price of seed goes up every year along with everything else. Even more important to you is that home-saved seed, if well done, is fresher and has

greater vitality. It's from *your* garden. And if you continue to save seed, the chances are, as the years go by, that your plants will be better adapted to your site and hence, healthier and more productive.

But saving seed is deceptively easy. If at the end of the winter you reach the end of the leek row and the five that are left are beginning to bolt, you might be tempted to say, "Oh, well, I'll save them for seed." Doing it that way, you get a pig in a poke. You should start the process by reading what you can about saving seed.[1] Then carefully consider what to start with. Say it is leeks. Start the process in the fall by going over the leeks and picking the ones that you think are best. Mark these so you won't eat them by mistake. As leeks are cross pollinated you will want to save a fair number, say ten or fifteen. (This will give you more seed than you need, but you can always share it.) Watch how they do through the winter weather. If their performance is as good as their looks, then save them for seed. Because of weed and cultivation problems, it is best to transplant them in late February to a spot on the edge of the garden, or even to a flower bed where they can be admired. Plants in the process of going to seed are usually wider and taller than when in the vegetative state. They often need to be staked. In late summer when you can see the dry black seeds within the husks of the flower you can shake them out into a basket or bag and bring them into the house for final drying. And there you are with your own leek seed!

1. The following pamphlets are good: *Growing Garden Seeds.* Rob Johnston, Jr. 1983 2nd Edition. Available from Johnny's Selected Seeds. $2.50 postpaid. *Vegetable and Herb Seed Growing.* Douglas C. Miller. 1977. Bullkill Creek Publishing, Hershey, Michigan. $3.25.

Timing

The question of when to sow different plants so that they are in a proper condition for fall, winter or early spring harvest is a complex one. Each winter variety has its own requirements. Parsnips and leeks, typical slow growing biennials, must be sown early in the spring to have time to reach maturity; spinach and Chinese cabbage, typical winter annuals, need to be sown late enough in the summer so they don't bolt, but early enough to put on good growth. Kales, carrots and beets are sown in June and July.

The chart below gives an idea of the general timing needed on cold hardy crops. As you will notice, some of the most valuable winter vegetables are sown in July and August, which is already a busy time with harvest, vacations, and other summer activities. But if you want these crops you will need to plan ahead and save time to prepare the beds, sow the seed, and keep the plants watered and weeded. It helps to just choose a *few* of the more basic types to start off. After you get the hang of it you can expand! Of course, you can cut out *some* of the preserving of summer crops; winter cabbages and leeks mean less frozen beans or corn needed for winter meals.

Another aspect to be considered in the timing of winter crops is your climate zone. This is determined by your latitude, topograhy, closeness to large bodies of water, and general weather patterns. The best and most complete discussion of zones for the western U.S. is in the *Sunset New Western Garden Book*. It covers the area from California up to the northern border of Washington. I only wish the authors had extended their map another thirty miles north to include the Fraser River Valley of British Columbia, which is the last substantial agricultural valley before Alaska. This general area includes the city of Vancouver and Vancouver Island and is mostly zones 4 and 5. A great deal of winter cropping is possible here, and in fact is practiced, both commercially and by home gardeners.

Knowing your climate zone gives you some *general* idea of what you can grow and when you can sow it. But within each zone, though there may be similarities of temperature readings at any given point of the year, there will often be differences in rain fall, cloud cover, and amounts of wind. For example, zone 5 on the coast of Washington is a lot wetter and windier than zone 5 along Puget Sound or the San Juan Islands. Coastal growers might be troubled more by rotting of early seeds and, later, of mature plants. Their cold frames should be designed to protect against frequent rainfall and high wind. In these coastal gardens, although the winter frosts are less severe, the overall summer temperatures are cooler, and plants need a longer time to reach maturity.

Inland in zone 4 the frosts are harder, last later into the spring, and begin earlier in the fall. But, at least at lower elevations, the days are warmer in the summer, so plants can come to maturity

Timing for Winter Crop Sowing

JAN	FEB	MAR	APRIL	MAY	JUNE

In coldframe
or cloches

____	Beets	_____	Cabbage tribe*	__	Cauliflower _____
____	Bok Choy ____/	Leeks _____/		Chicory _____
____	Carrots	_____	Parsnips_____/	Endive _____
____	Coriander ____	Salsify _____/		Florence Fennel ____
____	Cress_____/			
____	Favas_____/			Keeper Beets _____
____	Lettuce _____			Keeper Carrots ____/
____	Peas_____	In flats:		Rutabagas _____/
____	Rocket _____/	Celery _____/		Swiss Chard _____
____	Spinach _____	Celeriac_____/		Transplant:
____	Turnips_____/			Cabbage tribe

*The timing for sowing the main crop of the cabbage tribe should depend upon Rootfly egg-laying in your district. See Sharecroppers for how to determine this. Transplanting is approximately a month later

Celery
Celeraic
Leeks

as soon, or even sooner. At higher elevations the season is shorter, and the frosts and snow cover is greater, making a climate suited to only the quickest and hardiest of winter crops.

Oregon has a similar pattern. The slightly warmer Willamette Valley allows for crops to be sown a week or two earlier in the spring than in northern Washington, and a week or two later in the summer and fall. South, in the Rogue Valley, zonation becomes a hodgepodge of local climates induced by diverse weather patterns and topography.[1] If all this seems confusing to you, don't despair! You can probably figure out what to do from your own experiments and with the aid of other gardeners.

In fact, wherever you live there are probably local resources. Lively extension agents or Master Gardeners may be helpful. Local chapters of Tilth (see Organizations) and other gardening groups may have experimented with extending the season of crop production. Books written in your area are always useful, and

Timing for Winter Crop Sowing

JULY	AUGUST	SEPTEMBER	OCTOBER
Chinese Cab _____/	Corn Salad_____/	Garlic _____	
Endive _____/	Radish _____	Onion Sets __	
Fall Lettuce_____/	Spinach _____/	Favas _____	
Florence Fennel			
Kohlrabi			
Keeper Carrots			
Radish _____	In coldframe		
Rutabegas _____/	Cabbage _____/		
Siberian Kale_____/	Coriander_____		
Turnips _____/	Lettuce _____/		
Over Wintering	Mustards _____/		
Onions _____/	Radish _____/		
	Rocket _____/		
	Spinach _____/		

_____ extension of sowing time
___ _ _ last time for sowing

last but not least, seed companies will give a good idea of when they sow certain winter crops. The way to adjust those timings to your site is to do a few succession plantings and *keep good notes.* If you do this, in three or four years you will have a good sense of your winter crop timing.

One thing that confused *me* a lot when I first started winter gardening was that English seed catalogs suggested sowing various crops—brassicas, lettuces—a lot earlier than I was used to. When I tried their timing it didn't work out for me. The best I could figure out was that I was just enough further south and the climate was just enough warmer for the earlier dates not to work.

When you crop year-round, you put seeds in the ground eight months of the year. Keeping seeds and sowing dates straight is wearisome, and it helps to be organized. Keep your seed packets in an alphabetical file so you don't have to spend hours finding the winter lettuce or the kale seed. Keep a copy of sowing dates on your refrigerator to remind you when to plant what. I have taken to keeping a small cardboard box in an obvious place filled with the seeds for that month. (The boxes from the seed companies seem to be the right size and shape.) Here I also store tags and a marking crayon. If you take notes you can keep them in the box, too. Make life easy for yourself. Doing it this way may seem a bit mechanical, but I find that having this basic information on a chart rests my brain. It allows me more time to think about the other variables of gardening like watching the weather, or even what's going on in the rest of my life!

Watching the weather *is* another important step you can take towards knowing when to sow and transplant your vegetables. Scan the horizon frequently. Keep records (mental or on your calendar) of when the weather did what. Observe the length of wet and dry spells. Does the phase of the moon have an effect in your area? (In northwest Washington it often clears up or stops raining a few days before full moon.) Does it seem as though it's going to be an early, dry spring? A late, wet one? Place your bets and gamble in the garden.

1. The Rogue Valley Chapter of Tilth Association, c/o Judy Weiner, 348 Hussey Lane, Grants Pass, OR 97378, is a good source for local information. A good local magazine is Siskiyou Country, 10394 Takilma Road, Cave Junction, OR 97523. This is a bio-regional magazine focusing on the local economy, agriculture, land use and culture.

Waiting

Winter is shorter when you know a garden
and can still pull beets in early December.
Even, after everything's turned under
long nights are hours of rest, not death,
earned sleep after the land's labor

when kitchen tables bear seed packets,
almanacs, sketches,
when conversation
conjures up a tangled trellis of peas
before the first one plumps in a furrow.

That day apple twigs are already knobbier,
crocus tips slice old mulch,
                    February
is already spring.

Robins watch the hoe.

                    Jody Aliesan

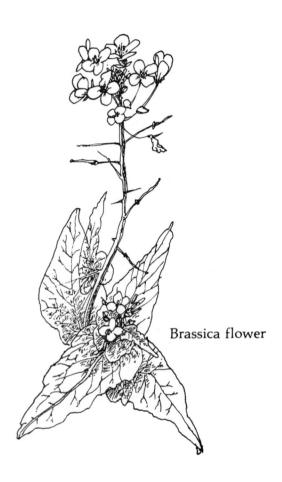

Brassica flower

Winter Gardening Mechanics

Starting Out

When you overwinter vegetables for the first time it's best to begin with just a few of the easiest and very hardiest. The list below will give you some idea of what to start with. I have arranged the vegetables by sowing date so you can plan ahead and fit them into your spring and summer sowing schedule.

If you live in an area that gets deep and extended cold spells, you can keep a pile of hay by the garden for mulching. Wherever you live, if the temperature drops below 25 °F and the forecast is for it to continue, mulch as soon as you can. By mulching over unfrozen soil you have the best chance of keeping the plants in good condition. Unfrozen soil also makes harvesting of the roots and leeks easier. All the vegetables listed below have, in my experience, survived to 5 °F with severe winds. Production, of course, stops until the weather improves, maybe February or March, but you are still *way* ahead of what any spring planting could do.

Beginners "Easy and Very Hardy List"

Month for Sowing	Vegetable	
April	Jerusalem Artichokes	
	Leeks	
	Parsley	Parsnips
	Salsify	Scallions
May-June	Kale	
	Savoy Cabbage**	Swiss Chard
August-September	Corn Salad*	
	Overwintering Onions	
	Spinach*	

*These are more productive if covered during December-March, unless winter is very mild.
**Ormskirk

Note: Although lettuce is easy, it's only "hardy." But the right varieties will survive to 5 °F under a frame. Look in the book *Salads The Year Round* (see Books You Should Read) for further suggestions.

Spacing

The spacing of hardy crops sometimes differs from that of the summer varieties of the same vegetable. An example is cauliflower. Fall and overwintering cauliflowers benefit from a spacing of 18 to 30 inches apart in the row or bed, whereas their summer counterparts can get by with 12 inches.

Naturally, spacing is somewhat dependent on soil fertility—the richer the soil the closer the plants, up to a point—but in general, plants that overwinter have time for more root growth and will produce a bigger plant if allowed. If you have a small family or a small garden and don't want huge leeks or monstrous spring cauliflowers, then you are better off to space a little tighter. Vegetables like lettuce, which are susceptible to leaf rot, benefit from the passage of air between the plants. Because of this, even plants such as the dwarf winter romaines, which could be grown cheek and jowl, should be given a little extra room.

Beds

I am of the opinion that winter crops, as well as most of the smaller summer ones, should be grown in wide row or bed style. There are several reasons for this. First, you get higher production per unit of ground. Second, you are not trampling on the soil around the roots. Third, the larger surface area of beds helps to warm the soil. And fourth, because the paths lower and compact as you walk on them, drainage off the beds improves.

Several modern books discuss this "new" intensive bed method,[1] but, actually, it has been in use for hundreds of years, both in Asia and in Europe. Salter, in *Know and Grow Vegetables*, reports that this was the method of growing vegetables in England before the Industrial Revolution lured the market garden laborers (mainly women and children) into the new factories. Then the farmers used the recently developed horse-drawn cultivation techniques and the single widely spaced row became the standard form. Gardeners soon copied it, and then it became the norm. Today, some commercial growers are reversing this process, taking their cue from the successes of bed gardeners and working out ways to create and weed beds on a machine scale.

Rotation

Crop rotation is an accepted practice with experienced gardeners and farmers. The main idea is simple: don't grow the same crop or ones of the same family in the same area two years in a row. This avoids concentrations of pests and diseases, and makes better use of the soil's resources. Because so many gardeners have been rotating crops in so many different situations for so long, there are many different systems and opinions about them.

After reading about rotations it's probably best to devise one of your own.[2] Year-round growing does make this process slightly more complex, but not unbearably so. I find it rather like three dimensional tic tac toe or chess. To keep it all clear I just make a map of the garden every year and try not to put a main crop (cabbage family, onion family, roots, corn, tomatoes, etc.) in the same place more than once every three years. Four is better if you can manage it. I also pay attention to the needs of each crop and try to suit them: high pH, low pH, high fertility, medium fertility, and so on. In fact, what crop follows what can somewhat be based on those criteria.

Typical 3-year rotation

Add organic manure	Add fertilizer and lime	Add fertilizer
Group A. Other crops	Group B. Brassicas	Group C. Root crops
Peas	Cabbage	Carrot
Beans	Cauliflower	Parsnip
Onions	Brussels sprout	Beetroot
Leeks	Broccoli	Potatoes
Lettuce	Swede	Tomatoes
Celery	Turnip	
Group sequence 1st year ABC	2nd year BCA	3rd year CAB

A typical English garden rotation system
from Know and Grow Vegetables 2

Don't confuse crop rotation with succession planting which means the planting of several different crops (say of lettuce) within the same season.

Winter Weeds

One result of year-round cropping is a whole new set of weeds. When you till in your garden in October and put it to bed with a green manure for the winter you don't have to worry about perennial and winter annual weeds. One fine day in March you till up the whole thing; when it's rotted down enough you till again, and then you commence to sow summer crops. Maybe you encounter some quack grass or a few thistles, but mostly you are dealing with summer annuals such as lambs quarters, pigweed and barnyard grass.

But if you have six to ten vegetable crops which are ready at different times from January through May, you can develop spotty areas of weeds that overwinter just as happily as your vegetables: cress, dock, chickweed, groundsel, various grasses, dandelions, mallow, geraniums . . . I could go on but I won't. One way to deal with this is with a thick mulch. Another is to make sure that the late cropping vegetables, such as cauliflowers, leeks, lettuce, and spinach, are all together in one spot. During the early fall and spring it pays to weed the beds and paths early and frequently. Then, in late May when the winter crops are done, you just have one big area that you can cultivate all at once. Sow it to green manure for the early part of the summer. Or if you are fallowing (see Soils) you can make this your fallow area.

1. *How to Grow More Vegetables*, John Jeavons, is perhaps most popular. I *don't* suggest you take his system as gospel, especially in the Northwest. John Seymour and others have recently jumped on his "bio-dynamic French intensive" bandwagon.
2. The following books have discussions on crop rotation: J. K. A. Bleasdale et al., *Know and Grow Vegetables 2* (this is probably the most succinct and best); P. Chan, *Better Vegetable Gardens the Chinese Way*; L. D. Hills, *Grow Your Own Fruits and Vegetables; and Organic Gardening*; W. E. Shewell-Cooper, *The Complete Vegetable Grower*; S. Solomon, *Organic Gardening West of the Cascades*; Thompson and Kelly, *Vegetable Crops*, 5th ed.

Picking Your Produce and Eating It

Harvesting winter crops is pretty straightforward. There are only a few things to remember. First, don't plant more than you can eat. You will have to allow some extra for frost damage, but it's not that much more. Second, learn to pick crops in their season. Cabbages are a good example. If you love savoys and have four different varieties due to crop in early fall, late fall, midwinter and late winter, just make sure you follow the pattern. Because they are faster growing, the fall ones will be overmature by Christmas and will suffer damage from heavy frosts and high rainfalls. When you go out into the garden to get one for supper, look over the selection and take the poorest looking one first; the healthier, more vigorous specimens will last longer.

With the winter annuals such as spinach, lettuce, and corn salad, which overwinter in the rosette form, make sure you pick the outer leaves rather than taking the whole plants. By doing this you stimulate new leaves from the core. Lettuce especially needs to have its old, disease-prone leaves removed even if you don't eat them. Late in March, however, or early April in the North, you will start to have an abundance of lettuce and other rosette plants and your spring sowings will be coming on soon. Then you can shift over to taking whole plants before they bolt to seed.

If you live in an area with frequent freezing spells, try not to pick from your garden when the plants are frozen solid unless you are going to cook and eat them right away. Like as not they will rot in your refrigerator. Do your harvesting when the mercury is above 32°F, and collect enough to last you for awhile. The salad greens keep well in plastic bags, parsley bunches in a small glass of water, and cabbages in any cool place. Don't overdo it though; vitamin levels drop daily in storage.

When you go out into the garden after a freeze or a bout of snow, it sometimes takes a little imagination to recognize a healthy red cabbage salad under some frosted, slimy leaves. Or a stirfry in those weird, elongated, almost flowering March Brussels sprouts. But just because supermarkets don't usually sell flowers for eating doesn't mean they aren't delicious. As for the cabbages, you can peel back the slimy leaves and throw them out just as well as the produce manager does.

Once you get to the kitchen many of the winter hardy plants may be new to you and your family, so it's important to seek out recipes that show them off to their best. If you overcook them or yield to the temptation to always serve them in the same way, they will quickly become boring. That path leads back to the supermarket bins of expensive, unvital vegetables. L. D. Hills has some good receipes, and Rombauer's *Joy of Cooking*, that marvelous kitchen standby, even has salsify recipes! And new cookbooks arrive all the time. The *Victory Garden Cookbook* is such a one. Written by a gardener it is organized by its vegetable ingredients. It even has three pages of celeraic recipes!

Substitution works well, too. If you can't find something new to do with kale, and it's all you've got left in the garden, just think of a gourmet sauce that's good over some other vegetable and use that.

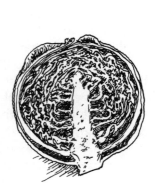
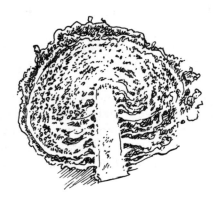

Self-Confidence

You might at first doubt that self-confidence could rate a place under Principles of Winter Gardening along with site, climate, or soil, but it certainly does. I became aware of this when I first started visiting other people's gardens. They would usually spend the first few minutes apologizing for the terrible condition of their plot, excusing the state of the broccolis, pardoning the peas, and generally assuming that there must be something wrong with their garden.

Many had spent the day before weeding it as if I was their relative inspecting the dust on their mantel, assuming for some strange reason that I never had weeds in my garden, or that my broccolis never failed, nor my peas ever shriveled. After I had written the first edition of *Winter Gardening*, another thing began to happen. People would say how much they enjoyed the book but then shamefacedly admit that they weren't growing very many winter vegetables! Well, that's okay! I assume that the *first* principle of gardening is that it is an art devoted to the feeding of a family *by* that family, and that, while you may or may not appreciate the aesthetics or routines of another's garden, if it feeds them, then how it looks hardly matters.

You should have the self-confidence to do whatever is right for you. For example, you may have decided that Brussels sprouts are too much trouble, that *you* don't want to stand outside bent over in the rain for ten minutes cutting those tiny little knobs off the main stem and then spend an additional twenty minutes in the kitchen pruning and cleaning them before cooking. In the same space you could have had a savoy cabbage, equally hardy, that you could have picked with one fell swoop of your knife and devoted but three minutes to cutting up and sauteeing for dinner. But if your neighbor loves Brussels sprouts and hates savoys, who's to argue?

Indeed, I have sometimes thought that gardening is rather like bushwacking in the mountains. There you are, contour map in hand, gear on your back, and setting off from the trailhead. Every once in a while, as you walk along you consult the map to see what that peak over there is, whether this stream has a name, and of course, how much farther you have to go. Then you come around a point of land and decide you'd like to try a short cut. It's at this point that you're on your own for a while. For a contour map is pretty general, and at 80-foot intervals it's not going to tell you much about the details, and you've just deumbilicalized yourself from the trail, so you have to rely on your senses. You are right there on the mountainside, with every stone and boulder, lichen and fir, flower at your foot and ice peak up ahead. If you can relax enough, you and the mountainside become the trail, your own trail, but also only one of the many trails in that field.

Alpine bushwacking is, of course, easy because of the view. Bushwacking down below in the firs and brush is another matter. Winter gardening is still pretty easy because the view is open. There aren't a lot of books and experts, like there are in summer gardening, grown up like firs and bushes, entangling your view.

Of course, most people think I'm an expert by this time. And I have filled all these pages with what I think I know. But it's just a contour map, and *you* will encounter the details. Also, it's hard to write about what I don't know when I don't know it yet! So have faith in your own abilities, and in the plants, and just go ahead and experiment!

> *"You should not lose your self-sufficient state of mind. This does not mean a closed mind, but actually an empty mind and a ready mind. If your mind is empty, it is always ready for anything; it is open to everything. In the beginner's mind there are many possibilities; in the expert's mind there are few."*
>
> Suzuki Roshi

Cloches
and
Frames

INTRODUCTION

Some of the best of the cold hardy crops benefit from protection by frames or cloches. In the fall these include lettuce, spinach, rocket, the immature overwintering European cabbages, and the leafy Asian brassicas. The very early spring plantings of peas, lettuce, carrots, beets, spinach, turnips, potatoes, and the cabbage tribe (broccolis, cabbages and cauliflowers, etc.) are all advanced about a month by the use of glass. A bit later on, the seed bed for leeks and annual flowers can be covered to advantage, and, of course, during the summer, frames can be used on heat-loving summer crops such as tomatoes, peppers and melons.

But like vegetable varieties, frames must be matched to their climate. Most Americans when hearing the words "cold frame" think promptly of the high-walled sort popular in continental climates that remain in a fixed spot in the garden. While these are good for starting flats of hardy plants or hardening off tender ones, they are not really suited to gardening year round in a maritime climate.

To my mind the best frames are *modular* ones that can be easily moved from one part of the garden to another to follow your successions and rotation of crops. In fact, I have made the beds in the part of the garden that gets most of the winter crops the length of five of my frames, so that I can cover a whole bed without any wasted space. This also helps me to estimate how much to plant: four frames of spinach, one of lettuce, one of turnips and other greens, etc. Very handy!

A reliable *venting system* is another necessity for frames in our climate. Ventilation is far more important than weather tightness in a maritime climate. If you look at a cold frame design from an East Coast or Midwestern book you will encounter all sorts of tricks—insulation, double glazing, heat storage—that, as far as I can see, are unnecessary or even harmful here. We have far more cloud cover and much warmer winters. If you were to grow lettuce at our low light levels, and at the high temperature, high humidity conditions that would result in an airtight frame, you would get leggy, weak plants and lots of fungal growth. Continental climate cold frames have to combat desiccating low temperatures, but they often have fair light levels, even at the winter solstice, due to the many sunny days and the highly reflective snow cover.

In mild falls it is important to leave cold frame covers off of the lettuce and spring cabbages. Light levels in November and December are quite low, and if the days are warm the plants will put on too much weak, sappy growth. If a hard freeze comes in late December or early January the plants will be too tender and succumb to frost, even with the covers back on. If you live in very cold areas it's a good idea to have some old rugs or mats to place on the frames during very hard freezes. A thick hay mulch will work too, though it is more of a bother.

Another important reason to have permanently opened vents or some automatic system set to a certain temperature, is the uncertainty of our weather. On those winter days when the sun comes out for an hour or so, temperatures can rise much more quickly in an enclosed space than outside. Since the average cloudy day in the maritime Northwest runs about 45 °F, it doesn't take too long in the sun to reach a point at which the plants, with their roots in cold soil, are suffering from evaporation stress.

Old books on frame gardening say that most venting should happen from the top of the frame or cloche so as not to cause a draft over the plants. An exception is on clear frozen mornings when venting from the bottom causes a slow warmup which allows the plants to thaw more gently.[1] If you have tunnel cloches you should vent from the top, never the ends, to avoid disastrous breezes through the tunnel. Because heat rises, top venting also utilizes natural convection. If possible, place your frames crossways to the wind and the area behind them will be sheltered also.

Another aspect of frame growing is the importance of watering. Many frames completely exclude rain, and even narrow cloches, which allow some moisture to seep into the soil beneath the covers, can get a very dry surface soil after a couple of weeks with low rainfall. If this happens in the spring, young plants of lettuce and bok choy, peas, etc., should be watered as needed.

Fall plantings are not in so much danger as they usually have bigger root systems, and the soil is wet by the time they are covered. But even they should be watched.

Almost all frames will need some form of *guying* or fastening against the wind. Few things are as disturbing as finding frames and broken glass all over your garden after a stormy night.

Listed at the end of this chapter are several good books, articles, and pamphlets on growing under frames. You can learn a fair amount from them, but you will have to work out your own schedule of what to grow and when to cover it.

In the next few pages I will discuss some of the types of frames and cloches that I have found useful (or not) in the last few years.

WALLS AND TERRACES

The simplest device to make into a warm microclimate is a south facing wall or terrace. Either can have window frames leant against them to shelter plants. A disadvantage of walls is that after the spring equinox they begin to lose sun; it begins to rise and set in the north. This makes walls best for the low-growing, quick winter annuals such as corn salad, lettuce, spinach, and some tender herbs such as rosemary. If the wall belongs to a building which has broad eves this site will also be quite dry—a plus in winter, a disadvantage in summer.

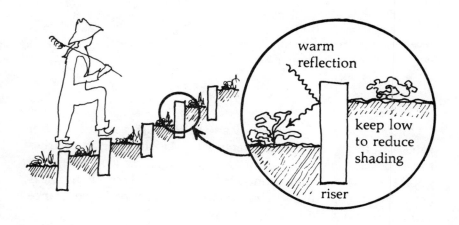

If you have a considerable slope, terraces are a fine way of gardening as they are well drained but more exposed to sun and rainfall. Remember that the warmest spot is right against the riser so don't put your path there.

CLOCHES

"Cloche" is a French word meaning bell, referring to the bell-shaped jars that were originally used as hot caps to put over tender plants early in the year to protect them from frost. The term expanded in meaning to include many different sizes and shapes of glass structures that could be put over individual plants in a row, or over the whole row (a barn or tent cloche), and then stored when not in use. Now some are available in fiberglass or other long-lasting synthetics, but they are quite expensive. Handy if you have the money though. Others you can make yourself for a small investment.

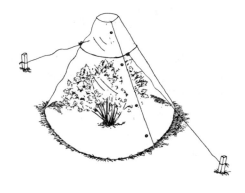

Fiberglass cone: A pattern for this is available from the developer, Solar Survival (see Organizations). It is handy to put over individual herbs or heat-loving plants such as eggplants, of which you may have only a few. Good for forcing rhubarb when covered with a dark cloth.

Bottle: You can find used plastic gallon jugs and cut the bottoms off them; they make temporary cloches for the earliest brassicas and cucurbits. Most are too small and opaque to be good for overwintering plants. When you use them on brassicas, cover the top opening with screening to prevent rooftly entrance. Watch for overheating and mildew.

Corrugated Fiber Glass: I haven't used this system, but Shewell-Cooper seems to like them. You will have to devise your own ventilation system: I would opt for cutting a series of small, permanent holes in the top. One real drawback is the need to remove the whole structure to work on the plants.

Cloch Wires and Clips: The making of cloches from panes of glass and specially constructed wires was developed by an Englishman named Chase in 1912. Modified only slightly since then, it has remained deservedly popular with gardeners and commercial growers ever since. When properly put together each cloche is rigid and can be moved as a unit. The top pane of glass can be removed to work on the crops underneath. Maximum width is 23 inches and the length is 24 inches. I don't know of any U.S. outlet (see Suppliers for a British one).

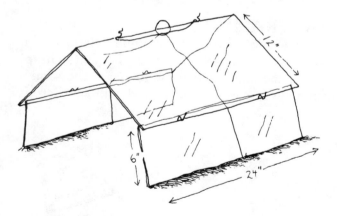

A more recent development is plastic clips to hold the glass instead of wires. These do not hold the panes of glass rigid, and are susceptible to wind damage. Furthermore, there is no quick and efficient way to remove the front pane when you want to weed, water, or pick crops. I don't recommend them.

CATERPILLARS, PODS, AND PUPTENTS

In recent years the National Center for Appropriate Technology has been testing and propagandizing various types of cold frames. They awarded grants to regional groups to test old types, to develop new ones and planting schemes to use in them, and to let the gardening public know about them. While many of the new cold frames are ingenious, none of them to my mind and experience are as useful and simple as the old types.[2]

Caterpillar: Constructed of wire or PVC pipe and heavy duty polyethylene plastic. Cheap, quick and easy to make, it is well suited to wide rows or beds. *Not* wind sturdy so best for cities and summer use. You can make a crawl-in size at extra expense.

Pod: This is a tunnel formed of fiberglass with solid plywood ends. It is sturdy and able to withstand winter winds, and not *too* heavy to carry around. Ventilation and access to plants are problems. All in all I wouldn't build one for my garden.

Puptent: A frame built in the shape of a low tent. The sides are covered with fiberglass or poly sheeting. They do not lift off and hence, ventilation and access to plants is, again, difficult.

OLD WINDOW FRAMES

If you have a source of old wood or aluminum windows you can construct two sorts of frames with them. They are cheap, easy to put together, modular (if the windows are the same), wind stable when guyed, easily vented, and will take crops

through some of the coldest winters we get. They also provide easy access to crops beneath them. The one disadvantage is that when set up in the tent form, the plants closest to the edge are a bit crowded by the inward leaning glass. If the panes break you can reglaze them with fiberglass. Fiberglass panes are lighter and always need guying systems in windy periods.

DUTCH LIGHTS

In the nineteenth century the French and then the Dutch market gardeners evolved the most practical and cheap modular structures for frame gardening. I don't think anyone has really improved on them for commercial scale growing.[3]

Dutch lights consist of low wooden rims or boards with the northern ones a few inches taller than the southern ones. These boards are the supports for long panes of glass which are fitted into treated or painted frames held in place by points or blocks of wood. No putty is used as it does not last well in the weather and makes glass replacement an unnecessarily tedious job.

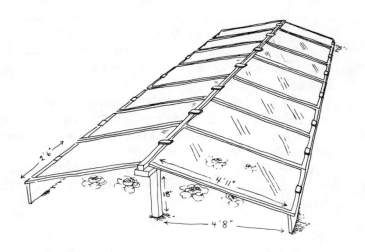

Dutch Lights: Ends are closed off with boards and held in place with stakes.

Access is achieved by removing a frame entirely, or by sliding it over on top of its neighbor. You ventilate by propping up the top or leeward side of the frame. Minor disadvantages are that the southern rim blocks some of the low winter sun and unless the wooden frames are narrow, access to the plants in the rear is a bit difficult. The European gardeners used boards between the rows or propped up over the plants to lean on as they did their work. Dutch lights are built in single or double form.

HOT BEDS

A hot bed is any kind of large cold frame with a pit dug under it and filled with manure. The manure decomposes and in the process generates heat and carbon dioxide, both useful to the plants in the bed. Horse manure is the best to use as it gives the longest lasting, most even heat.

Opinions differ as to the amount or depth of manure required to generate heat. Several people have reported to me that they don't get any heat unless they use three feet of manure. This seems like rather a lot. A very good book written by a commercial English gardener in 1913, *Intensive Culture of Vegetables: the French System,* calls for ten inches of well trodden horse manure and straw, *half old, half new.*[4] Make sure the manure is moist so that bacterial action can take place.

I have used as little as eight inches of horse manure under my late melon beds, but I didn't get much extra heat, maybe an extra 5°F. Friends who used two feet under a walk-in frame in Seattle got considerable heat in January.

About six to eight inches of soil goes on top of the manure, raising the bed to its normal level. You can then sow seeds or put in transplants.

1. *Intensive Salad Production.* C. P. Quarell. 1949. Crosby Lockwood & Son, Ltd. London.

   Very explicit and comprehensive directions for success in commercial production. Many directions of interest to gardeners also. Out of print; xerox available from Coolidge Center for price of xerox (see Northeast References).

2. *Coldframes and Cloches: Extending your Growing Season.* Willamette Community Design Center. 1981. P.O. Box 10273, Eugene, OR 97440.
   Pretty good booklet on frame growing for the Northwest.
   Coldframes: Four Season Production in Northwest Washington. Eric Van Valkenburg. 1981. Whatcom County Opportunity Council, P.O. Box 159, Bellingham, WA 98227. $1 plus postage.

3. In England some good commercial wide-bed frames have been developed called Access Frames. You can find photographs of them in *Basic Book of Cloche and Frame Gardening* by W. E. Shewell-Cooper. 1977. Barrie & Jenkins Ltd., 24 Highbury Crescent, London, England N5 1RX.
   This is one of the best and the most recent English books on types of frames and year-round use. Now out of print. If you find a second-hand copy, buy it!
   "Cold Frames and the Year Round Gardener," Carl Woestendiek, p. 8-9, Tilth, Fall 1981.

4. *Intensive Culture of Vegetables; the French System.* P. Aquitas. 1913. L. Upcott Gill, London.
   A 1978 reprint is available from Solar Survival Press (see Oganizations). Aside from the explicit hot bed building directions, this is a very detailed guide to intensive vegetable production under frames. Good photos and drawings in the general chapters. Eighty-two page monthly calendar of planting and other operations. Whole chapter on melon cultivation under frames. Well worth it for the devoted intensive gardener.
   American horticultural manuals from the same date recommend from 20 inches to two-and-a-half feet. The most the Aquitas book calls for is up to two feet for the February melon beds as these should not fall below 60 °F. I suppose this difference is due to climate; more manure is needed to generate sufficient heat in the colder continental climate of the East Coast of the United States than in maritime climates. In any case, most hardy vegetable seedlings will germinate and grow well with less heat. Some lettuce I sowed in January under window frames germinated at 50 °F. Quarrell says over 40 °F is acceptable.

Cloches and Frames References
Gardening Under Cover, William Head. 1983. Amity Foundation, P.O. Box 11048, Eugene, OR 97440. $9.50.
Salads the Year Round. Joy Larkcom. 1980. Hamlyn Publishing Group Ltd.
   Available from the Tilth Association, Seattle Chapter (see Organizations). A very good book by a happy vegetable fanatic. Full of good information. If you like salads you shouldn't be without it.

The Land Knows You're There

I know some people who live in the north,
They've lived there since Columbus, and many years before.
They live in the wilderness where few men go,
And they say that in that country no man can be alone.

> For the land knows you're there,
> The land knows you're there.
> And the rocks and trees and rivers
> Give you friendship and care.

Every rock and tree has its own true name,
And you tell them that you're coming as you pass thru the land.
You never can be lonely, alone though you may seem,
For a tree is like a person and it keeps you company.

You give a happy greeting when you come to a spring,
As if it were a relative or a long-lost friend.
And when you've sat and rested and you've drunk your fill,
You give the spring a "thank you" and a fond farewell.

When you come into a land that you have never known,
You bend and touch the soil and you tell it why you've come.
You tell it where you're going and you tell it where you've been,
And they say that if you're kind to it, the land will be your friend.

And when a man is old and his life is near an end,
He takes a final journey to say farewell to the land.
He tells it not to miss him and he tells it not to mourn
But to learn to live without him when he's dead and gone.

This northern land is healthy, on love and care it thrives,
But down in my hometown they've forgot the land's alive.
They've poisoned every river and they've leveled every hill,
But underneath the concrete the land is living still.

Leanne Hinton

Sharecroppers

INTRODUCTION

I haven't encountered too many pests or diseases during the actual winter. Slugs, mice, and rot are the main exceptions. But for the slow plants, ones that have to grow all summer to produce in the winter, there are indeed some formidable sharecroppers. Take-alls might be a better term!

When dealing with these pests I think it's useful to take the time to understand the organism, its life cycle, and its place in the local habitat. If you just run for the Raid can, *or* the Rotenone, you run the risk of breeding resistant pests. Even worse, you never get to understand *why* you have this pest and *if* you can change your gardening habits to reduce its predations to an insignificant minimum.

One way of dealing with pests in a coordinated manner is through a set of procedures referred to as Integrated Pest Management (IPM). What follows is a short outline of this method.[1]

The first step is to systematically check out what is happening. What sort of damage is occurring and on which plants? Is it happening at night or in the day? Can you see the culprits, or just their effect? (Perhaps a neighbor or your local Cooperative Extension Agent or a Master Gardener, can aid you in identifying the organisms.) Will your yield be decreased? How much? This sort of observation is called *monitoring*.

Once you have zeroed in on the pest organism, look at your yard and garden and figure out where the pest is hiding and if any of your gardening habits—or your ornamental vegetation—encourage or discourage the pest. Neatness and cleanliness are often next to pestlessness. If you can change any of these factors to discourage the pest, that's called *habitat manipulation*.

Sometimes *when* you plant a crop, or *how* you take care of it will increase or decrease the damage. So changing your gardening patterns—*cultural controls*—is a possibility. An example is waiting to transplant sensitive Brassicas until most of the cabbage rootflies have stopped laying eggs.

Encouraging pest predators—*biological controls*—is helpful

too, though this is often difficult and expensive for home gardeners. In the maritime Northwest we have many imported pests whose original habitats and predators got left behind. Sometimes there are local predators though, and you can spend some time observing them. Birds and syrphid flies belong in this category.[3] With reading and observation, you can learn to create habitats for the predators you want to have around.

You can also try to keep the pest organism from getting to the crop—*barriers*. What method you use depends upon whether it flies, crawls, burrows or slimes. Setting *traps* is often effective.

Finally, there is the use of *poisons,* whether "organic" botanicals such as rotenone, pyrethrum and derris, or the numerous and usually (though not always) more toxic "chemical" ones.

Basically, the IPM method takes a little extra time and attention on your part. It is not an instant solution. But then, instant solutions often have disastrous side effects. Better to observe carefully and continually, gather information, generate solutions, and act thoughtfully, and only to the extent necessary.

I should add here that there are organic growers, theorists and writers who adhere to the idea that pests do not attack healthy plants. They say that if the soil is in good tilth or balance, garden conditions are right, and the gardener is not guilty of mismanagement, a clean, productive garden will result with few if any, problems. I, myself, think that's a complex set of "ifs."

Certainly healthy, living soil and healthy plants are the best defense against disease and perhaps even predation, but often as not one inherits a garden site that is way out of balance, and one has little control over the practices of one's neighbors, let alone adjacent sections of the county or city. Further, it takes some time and a lot of work to develop garden patterns which work well in a given site. So don't despair, or feel guilty, or inadequate if you have some problems in your garden.

CABBAGE APHID

Cabbage aphids are gray, mealy looking critters that over-winter in colonies on the underside of leaves of mature brassica plants. In the early summer—May—right after you've set out your transplants, the mature ones fly around looking for hosts. If they land on the young brassicas, they crawl down into the center of the plants and start feeding and hatching new aphids. This causes the leaves to warp and curl around them so they are hard to eradicate. If not stopped they can permanently damage the plants.

Cabbage aphids are parasitized by a minute wasp whose off-spring feed within the bodies of the young, turning them into little golden mummies. If you see a high proportion of mummies to feeding aphids, you can assume that control is underway. Then you only need to give the seedlings or plants a boost with seaweed or manure teas or a mulch of partly aged manure. Other helpful predators of aphids are lacewing larvae, lady beetles and their larvae, and syrphid fly larvae. As the adults of the last of these prefer to feed on flowers of the Carrot family (Umbellifers), I make sure to let some umbellifers such as parsley, dill, cor-iander, etc., go to flower for them.

If you regularly overwinter kale, Purple Sprouting broccoli and hardy cauliflowers, the chances are strong that you are also overwintering colonies of mature aphids or eggs on your plants. You should either clear out these plants by the middle of May or spray them with a solution of Safers Insecticidal Soap, which has worked well for me. Reliable sources tell me that Malathion, though hardly desirable, is far less toxic in its immediate effects to you and the predators than the often recommended homemade, but acutely toxic, nicotine spray. However, recently reported studies on the long-term effects of Malathion and similar poisons on brain wave activity makes me want to stick with soap.[3]

If your new plants become infested with aphids during the summer months you can wipe them off with your fingers and just spray a little soap solution down into the center right around the growing tip. Some hot, dry summers encourage aphids and you have to guard even the older plants. The aphid damaged leaves and stalks are susceptible to mold damage in later rainy weather.

CABBAGE BUTTERFLY AND MOTH

The larvae of a white butterfly, the Imported Cabbageworm, and of a moth, the Cabbage Looper, both eat holes in the leaves of cabbages and sometimes broccolis. They are sometimes a problem in western Washington.

There are at least two generations of the butterflies.[4] The first generation, in the spring, is not as intense as the late summer ones. I have only observed the larvae of the moth in the late summer. Both kinds of larvae can be picked off by hand, though as they hide down in the inner leaves they are hard to find. Holes in the leaves and little mounds of green droppings are signs that they are about. If you have more than a few plants and not much time, Thuricide or other *Bacillus thuringensis* preparations are useful. Bacillus thuringensis is a disease largely specific to butterfly and moth larvae.

As with most pests, it's best to treat for them when you have the problem, and you can see it's going to be serious. A few stray caterpillars on a well-developed plant won't hurt much, but on a young one they will.

CABBAGE ROOT FLY

The cabbage root fly maggot is a *real* impediment to the year-round gardener, as the crucifers, which it attacks, represent some of the hardiest and best of the winter crops.

The fall generation of the fly which devastates your Chinese cabbages, turnips and radishes as maggots, overwinters in small brown pupae in the soil not too far from the host plants. They are usually about three inches below the surface but can be as deep as five or six.

The pupae hatch out as dark gray flies, a bit smaller than a house fly, sometime in March or April depending on locale and the weather that year. In England egg laying time is related to the blooming time of Hedge Parsley *(Anthriscus)*, a member of the Umbellifera (Carrot) family and a food source for the adult fly.[5] As far as I can find out, no one has done studies to see what the flies live on locally. Dandelion is the only commonly blooming low plant at this time, and it is from a different family. Cherry blossoms perhaps? Maybe they don't feed!

For the first day or so after the flies emerge they are a bit slow and sit on the soil a lot, but after that you rarely see them unless you catch them in the act of laying eggs by your plants. After mating the female seeks out your cauliflowers, broccolis, radishes, etc., and lays her eggs in the earth by the stems. The eggs hatch into maggots which burrow down to the fine root hairs and commence eating. They feed for about a month, pupate, and then become the mid-summer generation of flies. In most places and seasons this generation is quite light and little damage occurs to June-July transplants. The fall generation, which usually starts laying right after the mid-August rains in Washington, is heavier, and a very high percentage of a young crop can be affected.

Maggots sometimes kill plants outright, but just as often they merely stunt them. Plants will look small, but normal to the inexperienced gardener, but then during sunny, dry spells they will all of a sudden wilt and keel over. If you then pull up the plants you will find the little white maggots have almost totally destroyed the roots and stem. The plants have just been sitting in the soil.

If it is a wet year some damaged plants manage to send out new roots from the stem above the area that has been damaged. However, if your plants have been too badly set back, they won't produce a crop, or at best a tiny one, and it's best to relegate them to the compost heap and put something else in their place.

The first element of protection against the fly is to ascertain the timing of the generations in your garden. To do this, monitor egg laying by setting out either cauliflowers or broccolis in early April and leaving a few of them unprotected. Then every day, starting on the second day after planting, carefully brush away the top one-half inch of soil within one to three inches of the stems to look for eggs. If you have transplanted properly—with the first leaves or cotyledons below soil level—then there is a lot of stem area before the root zone. Eggs will show up as a couple of very small, white, cocoon-shaped things about 1 mm in

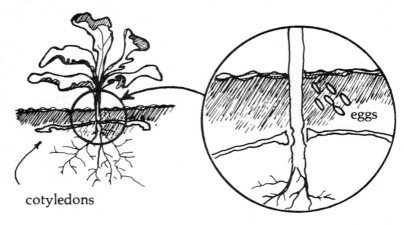

cotyledons

eggs

length. I simply pinch these out, putting the soil and eggs on the path where they will dry out and die. In my experience, the eggs have only been a short distance beneath the soil and it isn't necessary to disturb the roots when you do this. You can water them afterwards with fish or seaweed emulsion if you think your plants need it.

If you start looking just as the flies start laying, you will see only a few eggs at first. In a week or so there may be as many as twelve. These higher numbers continue for a week or so, and then there is a sudden drop to two or three again. Then you know that the laying is about to stop.

You should keep track of the laying cycle this way for two or three years and make some effort to correlate it to the rest of the environment—early or late, dry or wet season, plants in bloom, etc. If you do this you will have an idea of the egg-laying patterns of the flies in your area and you can time your main crop brassica sowings to avoid peak laying. This is probably the very best of

Cabbage Root Fly Egg-Laying Chart

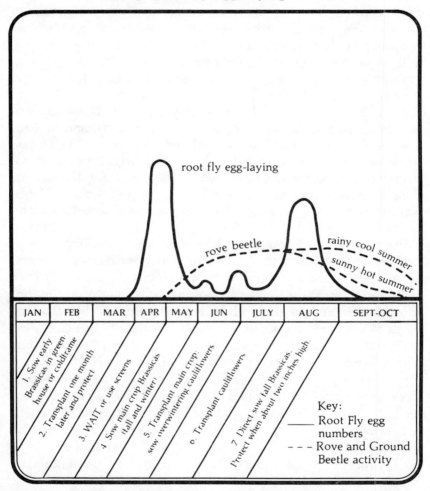

Note: the timing for when the fly mates and lays eggs differs from one district to another. You have to check the egg numbers each spring to determine this (see text).

the cultural control methods, and allows you to get most of your fall and winter brassicas off and growing with a very minimum of damage (see chart). Another technique that uses timing is to sow brassicas in September after the last of the August egg-laying, and overwinter them under cold frames, or in mild areas, out in rows or beds. There are specific varieties of cabbage for this purpose (see Vegetable List).

However, you will still have to protect your early spring sowings of cabbages, broccolis, turnips, and mustards, and of your late summer sowings of brassica leaf and root crops. To give you some idea of how to do this I will run through a list of methods people have developed to deal with rootfly maggot and discuss their feasibility and success. Or lack of it! You will no doubt want to choose the ones best suited to your gardening habits and crops.

Placing ashes around transplants and along seedling rows is perhaps the most common barrier method reported by gardeners. What's more, those who use it are convinced it works. My own trials and those at the Research Station in Puyallup, Washington, show that there is a slight effect against maggots, but that the ashes can corrode the stems of tender transplants (see Checking Your Results). Ashes must also be replaced after rains or waterings. Once a transplant is established and the stem has toughened up, ashes might be very effective as long as the fly has not already laid eggs by the plant. I have not tried ashes on direct seeded crops such as turnips and radishes, but reports are varied.

Another popular barrier is sawdust. Although it may be beneficial as a mulch, I have not found it effective as a barrier to egg-laying and, hence, maggot damage. However, others think it is!

Tar paper barriers, another barrier form, are, I think, plain nonsense. They often blow away, and anyhow the holes around the stems of the transplants are almost always large enough to allow the fly to insert her ovipositer right into the soil. In tests I did I almost always found as many eggs underneath the collars as in the soil around unprotected plants. A similar technique, developed at the National Vegetable Research Station (NVRS) in

England,[7] is to surround the plant with a compressible substance such as foam carpet-underlay. This fits fairly snugly around the stem of the transplants and also acts as a mulch that keeps the root hairs moist and is a hiding place for predators. These foam collars should be made at least six inches in diameter. The idea here is that the fly, if thwarted in laying eggs next to the stem will lay them further out. Hopefully by the time the roots reach the edge of the foam the plants will be big enough to withstand maggot damage.

I tried two kinds of foam collars in the spring of 1982 on broccolis, cauliflowers, and cabbages (about 30 plants in all). While the egg laying was heavy, I found large numbers of eggs around the stem of the protected plants (as well as around the controls), and under the foam on the surface of the soil. These were easier to remove than the other eggs because you didn't have to hunt through the soil for them. Perhaps they might be easier for the Rove and Carabid beetles to find, too.

At the very end of the laying period a large percentage of the eggs apparently hatched out and within two weeks most of the cauliflowers and some of the broccolis were dwarfed and died. Most of the broccolis (which had been good strong plants 15 inches in height) produced only small heads. I wonder how the National Vegetable Research Station had such good luck with this technique? Maybe a difference in the foam? Maybe an important factor was that the spring was cool, clear, and dry. Plant development was generally retarded and the fly activity was a good two weeks later than usual in my garden.

Both the Henry Doubleday Research Association and the NVRS report success with the cottage cheese carton technique. I have not tried this, but it apparently works by creating a dark space around the base of the plant in which the flies will not lay their eggs.

Root Fly
Control

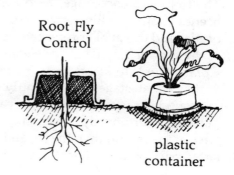

plastic
container

Now most of the above techniques are suitable only for transplants and don't work for rows of seeded radishes or turnips. Screened beds are a more suitable barrier technique for these and other seedling brassicas, and even for transplants. It works well if there was no immediately previous crop of infested brassicas in the soil. There shouldn't be if you are rotating your crops!

Fly screening from the hardware store, tent netting, cheesecloth (at least 16 threads per inch) or muslin all work well. These should be placed over frames which you can make of wood, wires, or PVC pipe. If you use the caterpillar type of cold frame then you can simply take off the plastic at the right time and replace it with screening. You *must* be careful to make sure there are no holes or gaps through which the flies can crawl. I place boards on the screening all around the edge of the bed and then cover it with soil. In very rainy or cloudy springs it is possible that the plants will not get enough sun to grow as well as one would like. But generally they will do better than if infested with maggots.

Tent netting has been *my* favorite and most successful barrier control against rootfly maggots. In 1981 (and following years) my spring mustards were absolutely undamaged. They grew luxuriently under the screening in spite of drought. Watering, weeding, and picking them was no problem. The years I have used screening on broccolis I have had excellent results as long as I was careful to leave no gaps at ground level.

In the area of biological controls there are several things to try. The first is to encourage the presence of the predacious ground beetles, both the big fiery searcher or coach beetles, the tiger beetles and the smaller rove beetles. There are good pictures of all of these in the *Rodale Color Handbook of Garden Insects* and the *Golden Guide to Insect Pests*. You should learn to recognize them as they eat all stages of the rootfly except the fly itself. The roves are especially useful in this job, eating many maggots, eggs and pupae. Unfortunately, like many predators, they often emerge later in the season than the fly and thus are better at handling the latter part of the infestations. They are encouraged by ample organic matter, but then, so apparently are the flies.

In March when the robins and other ground feeding birds return, you can dig up the soil in all the areas where you had brassicas the preceding summer, fall and winter. Leave it like this for awhile. The birds will feed on the worms and pupae and any other grubs they can find.

A relatively new predator to experiment with are the caterpillar nematodes. These are parasitic on soil larvae, apparently those of the fly family as well as the beetles and moths. So far all the university tests I've heard about have been done in California, but many gardeners are starting to try them in this area.[11] Some local gardeners have reported good results, others not so good. I tried them on my Chinese cabbage and fall broccoli several times and the results were not fantastic. But then, I have a fairly heavy clay soil, and apparently the nematodes don't migrate as well in clay and heavy silt loams. It seems that at best that control is a question of percentages. You get less maggots and, hence, less damage, but you do still get some.

Well, that covers what I know about control of the Cabbage Rootfly maggot!

CARROT RUST FLY

This small fly is a relative of the cabbage root fly and has a similar life cycle. During the early spring (usually April) the adult female lays her eggs in the soil by young carrots. The maggots hatch out and burrow down to the tap root and eat it and the root hairs off. These damaged carrots either don't develop or are stunted.

The maggots pupate through the summer and hatch out in August to go through the process again on the late crops. In some seasons and places there is an even later hatching in October. Damage from the last two cycles is largely in the form of burrows into the carrot's main root. These have a rusty color which is hard to see on carrots but stands out on parsnips, celery, and parsley roots, which the maggots also eat.

Strong efforts should be made to control the first generation of flies as the number of larvae that hatch out determines the size of the next generation. This is the one that is so destructive to your winter storage carrots. Some gardeners have reported that raising the alkalinity of the soil with ashes, limestone, or agricultural lime is helpful in protecting the early crops. I can't see exactly why this would deter the maggots. Diatomaceous earth is said to help, too. I haven't done any controlled tests with these materials. If you use them, work them into the rows before sowing.

I've heard that commercial farmers in Europe use mosquito netting or cheesecloth on beds of carrots. This does prevent entrance, but it also shades the crop, perhaps detrimental in cloudy springs, but a help in dry sunny periods.

Sowings after the end of May are usually free of carrot rust flies until the end of August, although you should check this out for your own site. If you time your winter storage carrots to be ripe before the fall maggots hatch, then lift them and store in a cool, damp situation and you will have next to no damage. The later you harvest carrots in an infested patch, the more damage you will have.

There is no doubt that carrots overwintered in well-drained soil taste best, though those stored in damp sand are almost as good. If you don't want to dig your carrots all at once, or don't have proper storage facilities you could try mulching with hay and then covering with plastic. If you do this right after you have removed the protective screening it seems you would avoid egg laying and, hence, damage. I haven't tried this but I have seen pictures from the Institute for Biological Husbandry in Europe showing this technique being practiced, so I presume it is effective.

In any case, leaving carrots *unprotected* and undug only breeds more flies for you to deal with in coming years. Mice and slugs like carrots also, and can do quite a bit of damage to the tops through the winter.

Another effective cultural control is to remove the wild Umbellifers (carrot family) in your neighborhood. Carrot fly maggots eat and overwinter by Queen Anne's Lace, hemlock, and wild parsnip. Their eradication can have a considerable effect as the adult flies to not go much more than a mile from where they hatch to seek hosts. Sad to lose those beautiful Queen Anne's Lace flowers though!

LETTUCE ROOT APHID

Local entomologists have told me that these are not really a problem in western Washington, but when I have shown slides of these gray, mealy aphids, which attack the roots of lettuce and are only seen when you dig up the plants, gardeners say, "Oh, so that's what that is." So they do trouble some gardens, and it's the late summer and fall lettuce crops that are most affected.

This kind of aphid lives on poplars that grow along the rivers and in low, moist areas. During the summer, adult aphids are blown by the wind into your garden. They then burrow into the soil and live around the roots of the lettuces, weakening the plants. If you have found them to be a serious problem there are several resistant varieties developed in Europe.[8]

SLUGS

Slugs like cool temperatures and high humidity. They are most active in the fall, when you are trying to get the late plantings of hardy crops up and growing, and in the spring when you're doing the same with the late spring crops. These are also the times when they lay their little pearl-like eggs under boards, decaying matter, and in garden debris.

Most varieties of slugs are scavengers and scroungers, preferring wilted, dying vegetation and young new stuff. The main reason they devastate your seedlings is that there isn't much else around to eat, especially if you have bare plots of soil with a few tiny plants. There are, unfortunately, a few important exceptions, such as the omniverous little gray slugs which eat anything, any time. Also, slugs in general seem to prefer cabbages, pansies, marigolds, and young squash and cucumbers.

I found that in the city, slugs abound in greater numbers than in the country. There are so many dark, damp tangles of ivy, clematis, brambles and garbage-filled trash barrels—slug heaven! Even so, I could keep the predations down to a reasonable level by getting discarded outer cabbage and lettuce leaves at my local grocery, and spreading them down the rows or on the edges of the beds. At night I would go out with a flashlight and pick up slugs before retiring. Same thing at dawn. During the day the slugs hid under the leaves so I got them that way also. This helped, but I had to keep at it. An interesting pamphlet from the Henry Doubleday Research Association, *Slugs & the Gardener*, indicates that you could catch slugs in your garden every night for a year and not make a dent in the neighborhood population. These mollusks are migratory and you would have to organize your whole neighborhood into slug patrols. (Not a bad idea!)

Or you could turn the patrolling over to ducks. Ducks are very fond of slugs. They have a special technique of bill-probing in grass and other vegetation to ferret out low-lying slugs that is very satisfying to watch. Ducks are also friendly, amusing, egg-laying and good tasting, and they fertilize rather than poison the environment.

In terms of the total picture, ducks don't consume much, if any, nonrenewable energy (none if you let the hens hatch out their own children), and so you are using one more or less self-maintaining animal to control another.

If you have a small yard and your ducks show too much of a liking for your garden vegetables, try feeding them greens before you let them in the garden. If this doesn't work, put up a fence and then just use them to patrol the rest of the property, and *you* de-slug the garden. The ducks will still be worth it due to that migratory tendency of slugs.

If you have a large country garden and don't like ducks there is always Deadline (metaldehyde liquid). This can be squirted from a plastic squeeze bottle along hedge borders or around precious plants. Though safer than particulate bait, it can cause serious gastric distress to larger animals that eat it or the slugs poisoned by it, so be cautious. So, if you have been using metaldehyde or other slug poisons on your property anywhere, you are in danger of losing your ducks! Metaldehyde is poisonous to them and will, at the very least, give them a severe stomach ache.

Ducks, of course, are better suited to suburban and rural properties than they are to most city ones, so city dwellers might want to use other forms of control.

Interestingly enough garter snakes are also slug predators, though they also consume toads, which are another pest control. Probably the balance is in favor of the snakes, so leave them be. Hedgehogs eat slugs too, but they aren't native to this country. Maybe, if you are enterprising, you could rent one from a zoo. Chickens don't really seem to relish slugs, but they will scratch up and eat their eggs if you let them into the *fallow* areas of the garden.

One useful thing is to mulch low-lying vegetables like lettuce with substances slugs don't like to hide under. Wood shavings are good. Hardwoods are best if you can get them. Sawdust or wood shaving paths and strips around the whole garden are barriers which many gardeners report help decrease populations in the garden itself. Recent Washington State University research has not demonstrated the effectiveness of this method however.

I never had any success with the stale-beer-in-a-cup method. Due to the rains, it seems it wouldn't be good in the cool time of the year anyhow.

Another old trick for slugs is to lay down boards in the garden paths and turn them over every day and stomp on the slugs. I use pansy plants instead of boards; more aesthetic! Slugs love the flowers and hide in great numbers under the plants. I place them in herb beds and other strategic sites around the garden.

The recently developed slug fence seems like a good idea. It's based on the fact that slugs, like rock climbers, have trouble with overhangs. You can make it of flashing, gutters, or any thin sheet metal you have about.[9] Unfortunately, the larger your garden the harder it is to surround with a fence. But these slug fences might be very useful around cold frames which unfortunately extend the season for slugs as well as for plants. Quicklime is very effective around cold frames too, though it must be renewed after rain and heavy dews. It is good inside propagation boxes, but not too close to the plants.

Garden Side

Slug fence

I have to admit that I *like* slugs. I think they are beautiful, useful as scavengers and have a right to live, especially the native ones. But I need my garden produce, and I do protect my plants when necessary.

WESTERN BLACK FLEA BEETLE

Flea beetles are the small dark beetles with enlarged hind legs that leap up from tomato, potato, and cabbage plants when you touch or bend over them. They overwinter in garden trash and weeds and emerge in April or May to chew little round holes in your seedlings. Their eggs are small and so are the larvae, which will eat the roots and stems of crops and weeds. There are one or two generations a year.

Some sources say they are worse in wet years, but several years ago in one of the driest summers in Whatcom County, they devastated both my early and late brassica seedlings. They start on the cotyledons and then go on to the first true leaves, never giving the plants a chance.

If your potatoes, tomatoes, and cabbages follow plants that are not hosts for flea beetles, and the area is large enough to prevent them from coming in from the edges, you will have few problems with them.

I know of no barrier techniques, and I use Rotenone. It works well, but needs to be applied once a week at midsummer. It kills worms. Derris and pyrethrum are said to work, but it's hard to find a source for them. L. D. Hills has a good design for a sticky trolly that you can rc'l along the rows. The beetles leap up and get stuck. He says this has a more persistent effect than dusting.[10]

One local garden writer advocates doing nothing about flea beetle damage in order to encourage the survival of the fittest among your seedlings.[12] If I did that in my present garden I wouldn't end up with anything to transplant. But then the soil was recently pasture and it's a clay loam over hardpan, so not a very good growing site yet.

DISEASE

Various forms of rot are a hazard to winter crops. Cultural controls and resistant varieties, when available, are your best defense.

Root canker attacks parsnips when they grow too big in poorly drained soil during the winter. Canker resistant forms are available from Suttons and Chase in England. You can also sow parsnips later, or more thickly, to get smaller roots. Most important of all, use raised beds or other well drained areas for your root crops.

Cabbages, and even leeks, will get slimy exteriors after damage from frosts. This is not serious if the underlying tissue is healthy.

Lettuces, those fragile beings that seem so important to the salad-minded, are perhaps the most susceptible to rot. Downy Mildew (yellow blotches on the leaves) and Gray Mold (gray fungus and slime around the stem and bottom leaves) are two of the most important. Reports from organic gardeners in Europe say that volcanic ash or finely ground basalt are useful if spread on the soil in the seedling stage. Powdered garden sulfur has seemed to work the same way for me, but it only reduces the problem; it doesn't eliminate it. In some places where I have gardened, my lettuces were very healthy, so I suspect that soil chemistry or other factors are acting here. It is a good idea to keep lettuce plants well spaced and make sure the late summer and fall sowings are in well drained soil and that cold frames have constant and adequate ventilation.

Onions are very susceptible to Downy Mildew, and the perennial and overwintering types often suffer. Proper spacing in the seedling stage and prompt transplanting are some help. Maybe compost, and balanced soil are too, but the effect of these is more subtle, and I can't judge that yet.

CHECKING YOUR RESULTS

How do you know if your various antipest efforts are working? Many people report success with methods that don't work for other gardeners or researchers. How can *you* tell if your strategies are really effective, or whether the lack of pest or disease is not due to some other variable like the weather, your compost (or lack of it), or your new sprinkling system?

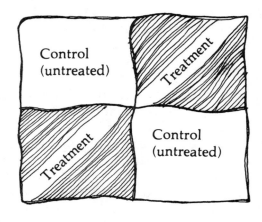

The standard method used by researchers is to try a new technique on a block of plants that are growing next to another block of plants, called controls, that don't have the new technique. The controls have been given the same care in every other way. Researchers have blocks like this in several parts of a field, or in several fields, and these are called replicates. The number of replications you do also adds information about the usefulness of a technique.

During the season you compare the treated plants and the controls, and if the technique seems to work one year, then you can try it for several more years to rule out climatic variables.[13] Here are three examples to give you some ideas.

Sawdust and Ashes as Barriers to Rootfly Maggot

In early May of 1978, my first summer in Whatcom County, I did a trial on the effect of sawdust and ashes in preventing maggot damage on cauliflowers. I bought 90 cauliflower plants from a market gardener and laid them out in a long bed as shown in the chart.

Sawdust Alone	Control (no treatment)	Ashes & Sawdust	Ashes Alone
28 Plants 0 Transplant Failures	19 Plants 2 Transplant Failures	22 Plants 5 Transplant Failures	21 Plants 6 Transplant Failures
8 dead or non-productive by maggot damage. 71% of plants productive.	7 dead or non-productive by maggot damage. 53% of plants productive.	2 dead or non-productive by maggot damage. 68% of plants productive.	1 dead or non-productive by maggot damage. 66% of plants productive.

This was a rather casual trial. I suppose I should have had several replicates in different parts of the garden, but even growing 90 cauliflowers took rather a lot of energy and space! The first thing to notice is that I was careless and didn't get an even number of plants in each block. That meant I had to do a little extra math to figure out percentages. The second thing to notice is that I had a very high transplant failure rate on those blocks with the ashes. This failure was visible the day after transplanting, and as I found the stems of the plants corroded, I presumed it had to do with the caustic effect of the ashes themselves, which I had piled up around the stems. A similar effect was also noted at the Western Washington Research Station in Puyallup at their trials.[14]

After this initial transplant loss however, there weren't as many losses from maggot activity in the ash and sawdust-ash groups as there were in the sawdust-alone and the control groups. I'm not exactly sure how to interpret this data, there are several possibilities. I think the experiment should be run again, redesigned. For one thing, when I started checking egg laying on the second day after transplanting, I never found many eggs. As it turned out later, this was about the time that egg laying drops off in this locale. The peak is usually in April.

If I *were* to redesign this experiment I would first of all do an earlier as well as a later sowing of plants. I would surround the stems of some of the transplants with paper to protect them from the ashes. I would make this tight enough to prevent the fly from crawling down it to lay her eggs. As soon as the stems were hardened I would remove it and pile up the ashes. That is quite a bit of extra work, of course, which is one reason I've settled on netting. I figure one procedure that protects a whole lot of plants at once is less work than fiddling with many plants many times.

A Slug Repellent Trial

This experiment was sent in by a Seattle Tilth member. I quote from his letter. The substance he was using was Fertosan Slug Destroyer. This is supposedly herbal, and is sold in Wales and England to repel slugs and prevent them from breeding. You can purchase it from the HDRA, but they say that gardeners have reported mixed results. The company will not release any information about it, and it isn't registered for use in the United States. When I need something of that sort I now use Deadline. I guess I prefer to use a low grade *known* poison to an unknown compound.

Dear Binda,

Well, I'm finally getting around to sending you a letter about my results with Fertosan Slug Destroyer. I have been waiting for the appearance of more slugs (our hard winter seemed to have really done them in this year) so I would have definitive results. The results are good.

My most recent test was to set out two saucers of beer (slugs love it) about 5 feet apart near my compost pile. Around one of the saucers I put Fertosan as directed to a radius of about 1.5 feet. The next day there were about a half-dozen slugs in the unprotected saucer and none in the protected saucer.

I got similar results in my potato patch. The

spuds usually have quite a problem with the small English slugs. With the use of Fertosan there were none of these pests in the plants though I did find them in nearby unprotected plants. The protection did seem to wear off after about 2 to 2½ months.

In general, I would say that the material works very well. I would, however, like some further assurance that the material is safe, it is after all a chemical.

Sincerely,
R. Aaron Falk

Companion Planting

This third example of an experiment to check out gardening theories is from the Henry Doubleday Research Association newsletters. The HDRA (see Organizations) is a membership organization for the purpose (among others) of research into and study of improved methods of organic gardening and farming. Each year they list in their winter newsletter, experiments which their members can undertake. You write in and get directions and seed or whatever. In the fall you report on your results. HDRA has members and local chapters all over the "British Isles," as well as overseas, so they get quite a lot of information this way. They also do experiments on their Trial Grounds at their center in Essex, England. In 1978 they commenced a series of trials to test the companionship effect of certain vegetables and herbs on each other as reported by Philbrick and Gregg in *Companion Plants* and repeated ad nauseum by gardening advisors and authors.[15]

To begin with they decided that they couldn't use the Latin Square so common for experimental plots of fertilizer or varietal trials (illustrated at head of section). Instead they planted a circle bed as used at the NVRS to work out the best distances between rows for new varieties. The idea here is that in the middle of the circle the two complementary (or uncomplementary) crops would be closest and have the greatest effect on each other, and at the perimeter they would be furthest apart and have the least effect. In one newsletter they reported on trying peas and garlic, a combination said by Philbrick and Gregg to be inhibiting to the peas. In later news-

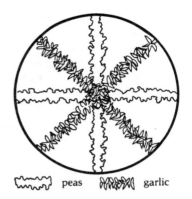

~~~~~~ peas   ~~~~~~ garlic

Circle Bed for testing the effect of increasing distance between two different vegetables.

letters the HDRA reported on trials with other combinations of vegetables, and some with herbs which supposedly had insect repellent effects. They also reported on work done by research scientists in Australia and the U.S. They tried out parallel rows of supposedly complementary crops such as beets and onions, cabbages and dill, etc.

In none of these reports by the HDRA or others were any of the effects (yields, insect infestations, etc.) numerically significant. The only exception was interplantings of vegetables with the herb Artemesia (Wormwood), one of the known and accepted allelopathic plants. Allelopathic plants have a negative effect, usually through root secretions on most other plants in the vicinity.[16]

My reaction to these reports is to guess that Philbrick and Greggs' original findings were idiosyncratic and that authors who repeat their information (without thorough trials) in books or other ways, are capitalizing on ill-founded information.

I'm not one to demand that everything be proven by "science." Quite the opposite. It's just that I get bored by hearing people endlessly repeat what plants "like" other plants without even crediting Philbrick and Gregg, who themselves request feedback from other gardeners on their experiences. Further, following those lists slavishly, instead of making your own experiments and observations in your own locale is quite contrary, I feel, to the practice of good gardening. Or good living.

What's more, my feelings about our common vegetables is that, since they are mostly derived from weeds which have associated with people and their manure heaps for thousands of years, they are by nature fairly flexible in their associations and, rather like city folk, can live cheek and jowl with their neighbors and not suffer unduly.

This is not to say, of course, that in their wild state they didn't form natural associations of mutual benefit; undoubtedly they did. I just don't know of any good botanical (ecological) studies on this. Besides, your garden, and the varieties you sow are not terribly close to the "wild" state.

> "Nothing exists but momentarily in its present form and color. One thing flows into another and cannot be grasped. Before the rain stops we hear a bird. Even under the heavy snow we see snowdrops and some new growth."
>
> Suzuki Roshi

1. Mostly derived from Helga Olkowski's *Management of the Pest Garden Slug.*

2. Importing predators is often useless as they simply migrate. But you should learn to recognize your local ones. The *Rodale Handbook of Garden Insects*, and *Beneficial Predators and Parasites found on Washington Crops* (Bul. #640) are good places to start. Unfortunately the Rodale Handbook is rather lacking in examples of major West Coast pests and predators. See also *Garden Insect Control without Synthetic Insecticides*, EM 3757 Washington State.

3. Safers Insecticidal Soap is registered as an insecticide and is available in garden and greenhouse supply stores. Basic H, liquid Joy, liquid Ivory, and vegetable soaps that are often found in co-ops and health food stores are not registered. However, they do work! One just isn't allowed by law to recommend them. Some detergents are phytotoxic (bad for plants), so it's

best not to use them. The information on Malathion was broadcast on National Public Radio during All Things Considered, in August 1983.

4. For good pictures of these guys look in the *Golden Guide to Insect Pests* or the *Rodale Handbook of Garden Pests*.

5. Bleasdale et al., p. 125.

6. Make sure to destroy any live maggots you find (check inside the stems also) as they are the next generation of flies!

7. Bleasadle et al., pp. 131-132.

8. Wisley *Handbook #28*, p. 23; Avon Defiance and Avon Crisp are two of the available types.

9. The original design for the slug fence consisted of hardware cloth, but small slugs can get through the spaces. Any sort of vegetation leaning against the fence will serve as a ladder for the slugs so clean cultivation is the rule!

10. L. D. Hills, *Grow Your Own Fruit and Vegetables*, pp. 144-145.

11. Available from Territorial Seed Company.

12. S. Solomon, *Organic Gardening West of the Cascades*, pp. 75-82.

13. *Improve Your Garden with Backyard Research*. Lois Levitan. 1980. Rodale Press. Emmaus, PA.
    The first chapter is the best part of this book to my mind. Better review it in the library or bookstore carefully. Still, it's the only book of this sort that I've seen for the lay gardener/researcher.

14. *Western Washington Gardener*, Aug. 1978, and personal communication.

15. *Companion Plants*. Helen Philbrick and Richard Gregg. St. George Book Service, Box 225, Spring Valley, NY 10977.

16. Henry Doubleday Research Association Newsletters: June 1978, Summer 1978, Autumn 1978, Summer 1979, Autumn 1979, etc.

Sharecropper References
Attracting Birds to Your Garden, Sunset Books, 1975.
   Fairly good coverage of Northwest species.

Beneficial Predators and Parasites Found on Washington Crops. 1975. Cooperative Extension: Washington State University. Bulletin #640.

Garden Insect Control without Synthetic Insecticides. May 1973. Cooperative Extension Service: Washington State University. EM 3757.

Vegetable Pests and Disorders. 1979. Wisley Handbook 28; Royal Horticultural Society. Audrey Books & Andrew Halstead.

Which
Vegetables
and
Herbs
to Grow

INTRODUCTION

I've tried to make the Vegetable List as comprehensive as possible so that you will be exposed to the full range of vegetables suitable for cool season cropping. I don't suggest you grow all of them, however, or even most of them in your first year. I haven't grown all of them myself, and I indicate when information comes from other folks or from books.

In most instances, I don't give general cultural requirements unless they are not available elsewhere. Not only am I trying to keep this book short, but I think that you benefit from reading *many* gardening books, especially the better ones. No one book says it all. Once you realize there is no "right" way to make a garden, then you are freer to experiment on your own.

NOMENCLATURE

The term "sow" refers to putting seed in the ground (or pot, flat, etc.). The term "plant" refers to putting a plant in the ground (transplanting).

I separated out the *Cruciferae* to begin the Vegetable List to make that group clear to you.

I experienced difficulty finding Latin names for some varieties, as many garden books and seed catalogs don't routinely list them. I did the best I could, though there probably are a few errors.

For taxonomy I referred to:

Oxford Book of Food Plants, Harrison, Masefield, & Wallis. 1969. Oxford University Press.

Wild Flowers of Britian & Northern Europe. 1974.

Grow Your Own Fruits & Vegetables. L. D. Hills. 1975. Faber & Faber, London.

The Tsang & Ma International Catalogue. 1977. California.

Flora of the Pacific Northwest. C. Leo Hitchcock and Arthur Cronquist. 1973. University of Washington Press, Seattle.

Hortus Third. L. H. Bailey. 1976. The MacMillan Co. New York. (The most "authoritative.")

HARDINESS

I have used the designations Very Hardy, Hardy and Half Hardy. Very Hardy are plants such as leeks, spinach, salsify, and corn salad that may live through temperatures as low as zero degrees Fahrenheit. Hardy are plants such as cabbages and onions that will mostly go through frosts of ten degrees Fahrenheit. Half Hardy are those plants that die at freezing or a little below (18 °F at the most). These designations are for the purposes of this book only; most of the plants mentioned are hardy compared to other garden vegetables. All freeze-out data are from maximum/minimum thermometers in my own and other gardens in the northwestern part of Washington state. Remember that these numbers are approximate. A temperature of 10 °F will cause greater damage if it lasts for three days than if it lasts for three hours. Several deep freezes during the winter will cause greater damage to your plants than one. A strong wind along with a low temperature will cause even greater damage. If it snows, and then plunges to 10 °F you will get less damage to the covered plants than if it freezes to the same degree without snow cover.

SOWING DATES

When discussing the time to sow certain varieties I often will say something like "June in the north, July in the south." By north I am referring to northern Washington and southern British Columbia; by south, mid-Oregon. There is about a month's difference in sowing and planting dates between these two locations which are approximately 300 miles apart. You will have to adjust these dates for your particular site. (If you live outside the maritime Northwest, see "What If You Don't Garden in the Maritime Northwest" in the appendix.)

SEED SOURCE ABBREVIATIONS

Where a variety is not well known or only available at one seed company, I include the appropriate seed company abbreviation in the listing. As seed companies shift inventory like any other business, this may change with the years. If a variety is presently carried by three or more companies I omit the listing.

ABL	Abundant Life Seed Foundation
BARBER	John Barber Ltd.
CHASE	Chase Compost Seeds
DAM	William Dam Seeds Ltd.
DEM	J. A. Demanchaux Co.
HAST	Hastings; Seedsmen to the South
JSS	Johnny's Selected Seeds
PARK	G. W. Park Seed Co.
RICHTER	Richter and Sons
RDWD	The Redwood City Seed Co.
SSE	The Seed Savers Exchange
STK	Stokes Seed Company
SUT	Suttons Seeds Ltd.
TER	Territorial Seed Co.
TILL	Tillinghast Seed Co.
SMITH	W. Smith and Son Ltd.
WELL	Wellsweep Herb Farm

VARIETIES

Many garden books won't even list varieties because they change so rapidly. The authors feel there is no point in recommending varieties that may be gone from the market in another ten years.

I have broken with this convention for several reasons. First, it helps to distinguish between summer and cool season versions of the same vegetable. Second, many breeders are switching over to producing hybrids and so, therefore, are wholesalers and retailers. Giving you the names of the best open-pollinated winter varieties will help you to recognize them when you find them in catalogs. If you purchase them now, you have some chance of getting to know them and learning how to save seed before they disappear. Although hybrids are not necessarily bad per se, and in fact a few are very superior, they are usually tightly controlled by the company that produces them and, therefore, expensive. Third, knowing the name of current varieties can give clues to the nature of future ones. If you read in a catalog under Celeriac, "Blanco—new strain developed from Balder for smoother ball-shaped roots and better uniformity," and you've grown Balder and liked it, you know that this new strain has a good chance of doing well in your garden.

My last, and perhaps main reason for listing varieties is that I hope to make the process of choosing winter garden crops a little easier for you than it was for me. I've spent ten years pouring over catalogs and trying out vegetables in my garden. Sometimes it was a bore to grow twenty-two kinds of cabbages and seven varieties of leeks all in one year, but it sure taught me a lot. The least I can do is pass on my impressions to you. And impressions is just what they are. At no time did I have the capital or time available to do the intensive kind of varietal trials that a funded research station or a seed company could do. Thus, my choices are often idiosyncratic and based on soil, local climate, taste buds, and how much attention I was paying to the matter each year while tending to my family and farm business.

If you are a beginner, it will help you to begin with some recommendations, though if you are reading this book ten years from now, you may find that catalogs look very different. The important thing to do is find the *equivalent* variety to do the job, whether it's an overwintering cabbage or a good coldframe lettuce.

CRUCIFERS

The *Cruciferae* group is so large and important to the year-round gardener that it merits its own section. Included in the group are *Brassica oleracea* (cabbages, broccolis, cauliflowers, and some kales), *Brassica pekinensis* (Pe-Tsai, Nappa, Chihili), *Brassica chinensis* (Bok Choy or Pak-Choi), *Brassica rapa* (turnip and some kales), and *Brassica napus* (rutabaga). Then there are the closely related radishes *(Raphanes sativus)*, horseradish *(Armoracia rusticana)*, rocket *(Eruca sativa)*, cress *(Lapidium sativum)*, watercress *(Nasturtium officionale)*, and winter or American cress *(Barbarea verna)*.

I list these not to overwhelm you, bore you, or impress you, but because they form a horticultural group. They have similar needs, pests, and diseases, and they have similar effects on the soil. When you practice a rotation, with a few exceptions, they should be considered as a group and *rotated together*.

The exceptions are watercress, which belongs in water or moist soil, horseradish, and winter cress which can go in permanent herb beds, and rocket, which is best grown as a catchcrop.

Our most important brassicas evolved in Northwest Europe, in the maritime climate there. Hence, they are adaptable to *our* maritime climate, and have special pertinence to this region.

Basically, most of the European brassicas are heavy nitrogen feeders, do well with lime, and are susceptible to attack by club root, cabbage moth and butterfly, cabbage root fly, and gray aphid. Most benefit from transplanting as it aids their root system. For individual preferences and cultural tips read Hills, Simons, and Shewell-Cooper (see Books You Should Read).

The Asian brassicas are a little harder to work with because their sensitivity to day lengths makes it necessary to plan their planting times carefully. But they are delicious and extremely useful for cold frame work in more severe climates. It's also harder to find cultural information on them. Hills, Simons and Solomon have some suggestions, as do the catalogs from Tsang

& Ma, Johnny's Selected Seeds, and Territorial catalogs. Chan's book is also helpful on some types, and the Horticultural Department at Rodale Press has put out a good pamphlet, *Summary of Cool Weather Crops for Solar Structures,* which discusses their use in frames and includes seed sources and recipes.

BROCCOLI

Brassica oleracea

Broccoli is one of America's favorite vegetables, and in the milder areas such as Seattle one can have it almost year round. Gardeners in colder sites will have to do without from early winter until spring. There are good varieties for each season, and you would do well to use them when they grow best.

Broccolis come in green, white, and purple (turns green when cooked). Their leaf shape and resprouting ability are their distinguishing characteristics. In England, winter cauliflowers were popularly known as broccoli, kale was known as borecole, and what we usually buy as broccoli in the store was known as Calabrese after the Calabrian region of Italy where those varieties originated. This, of course, led to a certain amount of confusion in nomenclature, and seed catalogs on different sides of the Atlantic would list the same variety under different headings. Since the establishment of variety legislation by the European Economic Community (EEC), however, this seems to have gotten straightened out. Cauliflowers are sold as such, and broccoli usually includes Calabrese types as well as the overwintering sprouting broccolis.

Summer and Fall Varieties
Hardy

Italian Green Sprouting
DeCicco
Waltham
Various hybrids

These belong to the Calabrese type we are all familiar with. In very mild locations such as Seattle they can be grown through the late fall and winter from July and August sowings. Frosts much below 18 °F do them in, and their heads are very susceptible to rot from rain. In colder districts you can have them until early December if it is a mild fall, but they need to be sown by June. They can also be sown in late January or early February under heated frames for an early spring crop.

Overwintering Varieties
Very Hardy

Purple Sprouting
White Sprouting (SUT)
Nine Star Perennial (SUT, BARBER)

These are sown in late May in the North, later in the South, and overwinter in the immature state to form heads in early spring. The Purple Sprouting are the best to my mind. They are very hardy, going down to 6 °F in my experience and withstanding Northeasters with much gallantry. They are *large* plants, taking up a good 30 inches either way, especially in March when they start to produce their small purple or white heads. The heads keep coming for a month or so, but get progressively smaller as time goes on. By the time they get as thin as asparagus you will be ready to turn them under.

This broccoli's only fault is that it harbors the gray cabbage aphid, which will then have ready access to your young, spring transplants. Chances of these colonies over-wintering are lessened if you spray the plants in the fall or early spring (see Sharecroppers).

I have not kept Nine Star Perennial over to see if it really lasts several years as the catalogs say. I don't know if it would be worth it as it would interfere with crop rotation and general garden organization.

BRUSSELS SPROUTS

B. oleracea var. *gemmifera*

Brussels sprouts, along with kale, parsnips and leeks, are the epitome of winter hardy vegetables. They are available from September till March, and in April you can eat the sprouts as they start to flower. They then taste much like broccoli and are good in stir fries. In fact, I think Brussels sprouts are better sauteed than steamed. They are also excellent in soups.

Early Varieties   Hardy

If you like to have a continuous supply of Brussels sprouts from September on, you can start off the season with some of the American types such as Jade Cross, Long Island and Catskill, or Early Dwarf Danish. Personally, I don't want to bother with picking sprouts in the early fall when there is such an abundance of cabbages. Also, for some reason I've not been able to get most of these types to grow well for me. The sprouts grow loose and since they are close to the ground and jam-packed together, maggots can come up from the root system in wet falls and tunnel into them. Their closeness also makes the sprouts vulnerable to rot, and they are not *really* hardy. Two more reasons not to grow them for the winter.

Midseason and Late Varieties   Very Hardy

Stickema (DAM)
Cambridge series (SUT)
Bedford series (SUT)
Roodnerf series (TER)
Hybrids: various new types

As a great deal of breeding work has been done lately with Brussels sprouts, it is getting hard to find the open pollinated varieties. The above list contains good series that have midseason and late types within them. They grow medium to tall in height: two to three-and-a-half feet. This allows the sprouts to be well-spaced along the stems; with none of them touching, this helps prevent rot. The sprouts are generally small and very tight. The English varieties, Cambridge and Bedford, tend to have bigger, elongated sprouts that have more of that disagreeable hot "cabbagy" taste.

I have been happiest with the Dutch-bred Roodnerfs. They are medium-tall and, hence, less inclined to lean over in the wind than the real giants. They have good-sized, hard, round sprouts of a very sweet flavor. They also seem more tolerant of poor growing conditions. Stiekema and Roodnerf Early Button are excellent midseason types; Roodnerf Rido and Late Supreme are good late ones. Rido is shorter and so perhaps better suited to windy areas. Suttons is still carrying the first two and Territorial the last. In 1982 Territorial was having Alf Christianson of Washington's Skagit Valley grow Late Supreme seed for them. They were selecting for taste, hardiness and wind resistance. I think that experienced gardeners would do well

to attempt saving seed of the other two varieties if they have the room and the inclination since Brussels sprouts respond strongly to environmental influences.

> *Brussels sprouts is a crop which shows very wide variation that is caused partly by the environmental and partly by genetic differences. This renders selection difficult, and in the past quite numerous commercial strains have failed to meet the requirements of all growers. As a consequence this crop, more than other cole crops, has been subjected to extensive selection by the growers themselves. The resulting growers' strains are sometimes adapted to the growing conditions in a certain locality. For instance, types selected on a heavy soil may show rank growth and produce loose sprouts when grown on light soils, and strains from a light soil may remain too short-stemmed on a heavy soil.*
>
> *Variety trials have shown that there are also strains that can be satisfactorily grown almost anywhere, and these are attractive to the trade.*
>
> *Cole Crops*
> *M. Nieuwhof, 1969. p. 79*

CABBAGES

B. oleracea

It is possible to have cabbages producing in your garden most of the year if you match variety with planting dates. Whether you want to eat that much cabbage is another question! I lose interest in them during the summer when there is so much else. But they are useful, very easy to grow, and taste so much better from your garden.

Early Spring Varieties   Hardy

These are quick little cabbages, usually with pointed heads, which are sown in September and early October, and *overwintered* in cold frames until they can be planted out in February or March. In some very mild districts you can overwinter them outside. They tend to be loose, and often bolt before they form much of a head, but they are tender, and because April to June is a period rather bereft of greens, I find them worth the effort. Jersey Wakefield, April (or April Monarch) and First Early Market are good varieties

Spring Cabbage

which are currently available in American catalogs. If you do well with these, there are others in the English catalogs to try.

One of the best things about these autumn-sown types is that they are too big and well established to be much affected by the rootfly maggot in the spring; a great bonus!

Green Cabbages for Standing and Storage

Very Hardy

I sow these, and the savoys and reds, in a seed bed in late April to early May (later in the South) for "main crop" cabbages. I use a seed bed because it's easier to keep them together for watering, feeding, and weeding.

I also sow the Brussels sprouts, late broccolis, fall purple cauliflowers, kale, and purple sprouting broccolis in this bed. And I leave part of it open for the overwintering cauliflowers which I sow a month later.

A month after sowing, I choose the best plants and put them out in their permanent beds. I usually try to soak the seedlings well the day before and to do my transplanting on grey, misty days, but if the weather doesn't oblige, I transplant at night and keep a fine spray on them during the hottest hours. The idea is not so much to make water available to their roots (which you're doing anyhow) but to keep the atmosphere around their leaves cool and moist. This way they are back to growing in a couple of days.

The heads are ready to eat in September or October but will stand in the garden until March in more or less good condition depending on weather and variety. I always leave the better looking ones for last.

As I live in Northeaster territory I also pull a few cabbages out by their roots and store them in a box or a heap in damp wood-shavings or sawdust. They keep fine this way under a shed, and even if they freeze, they thaw out with little or no damage. I also use them to make low salt kraut and Kim Chi in gallon jars and store it in the refrigerator when it has finished fermenting.[2]

My present favorites are Glory of Enkhuizen (JSS) for kraut, Christmas Drumhead (SUT), and Amager Green Storage (JSS). Christmas Drumhead is a small, loose cabbage, but in most years it stands very well. It has a delicate taste and texture, and its only fault is that it is extremely variable in quality. Amager is a heavy-headed ballhead type that is extremely hardy and stores well (Christmas Drumhead does not). It always seems to perform well in my garden in spite of my hard clay soil.

Red Cabbages   Very Hardy

Meteor, Mammoth Red Rock, the Red Storage cabbages from Stokes and the Langedijker Winterkeepers from DAM are all good fall and winter sorts. I haven't noticed much difference between these last varieties in terms of their ability (very good) to withstand rain, rot and freezes.

Savoy Cabbages

Very Hardy

Savoy cabbages are not well known in America, but I enjoy them more and more each year. They are loose, open cabbages and don't have a very long shelf life, probably a strong contributing factor to their lack of popularity. But they taste wonderful, have more greenness inside the head than other cabbages, and are certainly worthy of attention by the winter gardener and cook. They are also very beautiful. The old varieties are the hardiest of the cabbages and stand well in the rain and snow.

Their name comes from an area in northwestern Italy and is also used as an adjective to describe the intense crinkling of their leaves. This is thought to impart some extra hardiness to plants that have it (e.g., Cold Resistant Savoy spinach).

I find Chieftain to be an early sort and not really hardy where I garden. Ice Queen and Savoy King are a little better, but they are hybrids, and you can't save the seed. There have been attempts in the trade to breed savoys that store well, but I feel these are best ignored by the home gardener.

My favorite savoys are Kappertjes (DAM), which are small, very early ones for eating in September and October, and Ormskirk (SUT, TER), a standard English type that comes in autumn and winter forms. Ormskirk is super hardy and stands till March, or later in a wet, cold spring.

January King is another savoy. Before the European Economic Community rulings, it was just as often listed with the green cabbages, but now they have settled it as a Savoy. It has beautiful red tinges, and it's tough! (It stands the weather *and* takes longer cooking to soften up!)

CAULIFLOWER

B. oleracea botrytis

Growing summer cauliflowers has always been an arduous undertaking for me, but fall and overwintering ones are easier and rewarding. I treat them like cabbages, sowing the fall cauliflowers in the main crop cabbage seed bed and the over-wintering ones a month later in June. I transplant them out after a month and keep them good and moist till they get started.

If you are a beginning gardener, you might want to avoid cauliflowers in the first year and devote your space to a more productive and reliable crop. They are low in Vitamin A in comparison with other crucifers (though fair in other nutrients) and the winter varieties take up lots of space—three feet either way. If you do decide to grow them, make sure that you compost the soil well, that you keep them well watered in dry spells, and that you transplant them before they get crowded. Hills, Shewell-Cooper, and Seymour have interesting sections on cauliflowers in their books.

Fall Varieties   Hardy

These include types such as Purple Giant (DAM), Autumn Veitch, Self-Protecting Veitch, Dominant, and White Top. They are sown with the main crop cabbages and transplanted out with them. They are ready to eat by September and usually done by late November, depending on your locale. In a *very* mild location a slightly later sowing will give plants that crop on into December (I harvested Veitch Autumn Giant in January in my Seattle garden), and in English catalogs you can find varieties specifically for this time. I currently garden so far north that I don't experiment with them. (That doesn't mean *you* shouldn't!)

Overwintering Types Very Hardy

These are sown very late. I do it in June but the British Columbia research station starts them later and so do the farmers in the Skagit Valley. Must be something peculiar about my site or soil! If you want to try them, do some successional sowings through the summer to see what are the best dates for you. If I sow them much later than June and transplant in July, they not only get hit by drought, but devastated by Root Fly Maggot. Other growers probably direct sow and have been using insecticides and don't have to worry about this.

There are many varieties of these overwintering cauliflowers: the English Winters, the very fine Walcherins, the Armado series, etc. Unfortunately, they are not all available in American catalogs, and even British retail seed catalogs have nothing like the excellent selection that is available to the wholesale trade. Still, even with those available (SUT, TER, ABL) you can have fine crops from late February till June.

Another new cauliflower regularly grown commercially in the Skagit Valley is Inca, now available from Tillinghast Co. (see Seed Companies).

If you have a large family, you will want to put overwintering cauliflowers on 36-inch centers in beds. If you have a small family try 24 inches or else you won't be able to eat the monsters at one meal. In a good year the late April/early May ones are 18 inches across and if you have even two or three of those ripening at once you've got to trade or give them away. By June they are overwhelming. Planting at the later dates also reduces size.

CHINESE CABBAGE   Hardy

B. pekinensis var. *cylindrica*
All fall types

Chinese Cabbage, the big heading sort, is a plant which responds best to decreasing day length and temperatures. That makes it a good fall crop, and in mild localities, a winter one. But it's not so good for spring. I use one nonheading type and the bok choy types *(B. chinensis)* for late winter/early spring cold frame work (see Mustard section). I have had some Chinese cabbages last through January, when they start to flower. Of course, the flowers are as good in their own way as the heads.

The Chinese store their mature cylindrical cabbages through the winter in unheated adobe-like cold frames or in pits covered with mats. This keeps them blanched and in good condition.

Since they are sown in late summer, the plants are seriously bothered by the rootfly maggot, and it pays to make the effort to protect them one way or another. An extra-early sowing in late June or early July is well on its way before the mid-August maggot attacks. Unfortunately, in hot summers these have a tendency to bolt, so extra care must be taken to grow them in fertile soil with good irrigation. These later crops can be covered with screening or mulched with sawdust.

COLLARDS   Very Hardy

B. oleracea var. *acephala*
Vates
Georgia (HAST)
Cabbage Collards (HAST)

These small, open cabbages, very popular in the South and in black communities, are very useful as greens in the late winter. I have read that they were known as coleworts in England. I suspect, though, that both collards and coleworts were names for many different forms of small, loose, open-growing cabbages. I don't know which varieties have come down to us. Collards look very much like a primitive cabbage, and in the 30-odd plants that I've grown, I saw hints of kohlrabi, Marrowstem kale, red cabbage, etc.

Southeastern breeders have worked with collards more than anyone else as they are a winter staple there. They are grown commercially over much of the Piedmont area, and though often not harvestable during the depth of the winter, they are good late fall and early spring crops. In the Northwest a mid-July sowing will produce a good crop. They will go down to at least 15 °F, and most winters will be harvestable continuously, like kale.

CRESS

Barbarea verna Very Hardy
American Winter Cress (common weed, RICHT)

Lepidium sativum Half Hardy
Cress (RICHT, ABL)

You often find *Barbarea verna* (American Winter Cress) growing wild. In fact, it thoroughly naturalized itself in my old Seattle garden where I started it from seed one fall, and then ignored it because I found I didn't like it much. It tastes like a hot watercress. A small innocuous plant, it would do well in the herb garden where you could just let it be and gather small amounts for winter salads.

Lepidium sativum, the other cress, is more succulent and is often grown for sprouts (as well as in the garden) in Europe. Hills had a good description of how to do this under a cardboard box.

KALE

Very Hardy

B. oleracea
B. campestris

Kale, along with leeks, turnips, parsnips, and the hardiest cabbages, formed the mainstay of late winter vegetable eating for Northern Europeans for many centuries. In fact, according to John Seymour, gardens in Scotland (approximately 56° to 59° latitude) were known as Kailyards, which has interesting implications for coastal Alaskans.

Tall
Curled Kale

There are many varieties of kale that I have read about but not seen listed in catalogs: old standards of self-sufficient gardeners and farmers that have disappeared along with so many other varieties since the Industrial Revolution, with its freezers, trucking, and changes in eating patterns. But kale, though you might not find it in the supermarkets, is high in vitamins A, C, E and K, and being so hardy, merits your attention, if not midwinter devotion, and a place in your garden. The spring sprouts, tender and broccoli-like, are superb.

Hills says there are two forms of kale. The first stems from *B. oleracea*, and includes Dwarf and Tall Scotch, Semi-Dwarf and Tall Curled, and Thousand Headed (DAM). Thousand Headed is huge and used for stock. The others (which seem to me to be just one variety in tall and dwarf) can be started in May or June in flats or in the cabbage seed bed. They can then be set out at their normal spacing (24 inches between plants) a month later.

The second form of kale does not transplant well. It stems from *B. campestris* types and includes Siberian, Russian (ABL), Hungry Gap, and Asparagus kale.

B. campestris types can be sown directly in July or August at 18-inch spacing. If you are worried about germination, sow a few extra seeds and then thin, feeding the discards to the stock in September or eating them yourself. Unless your soil is awful, don't manure or fertilize before you sow; the plants will grow too fast and won't be as hardy.

I usually have about 3-6 plants of the tall curly kale, and two to three of the Siberian. I use the curled through March, when it starts to flower and I've cut all the sprouts of any size. Then I pull it up, turn in the soil, and turn my attention to the Siberian. It will last approximately another month in a cool spring.

I like Dwarf Siberian better for eating raw, especially in spring when the new sprouts and leaves are very tender. Some folks I know eat Scotch and the Green Curled varieties raw too, but I find them tough and strong flavored (except in the spring) even though they do improve after a few frosts. I prefer them in soups and stews where they are delicious. Russian kale and Cottagers are reddish-purple ones, and like Hungry Gap, taste mild like Siberian, even in the fall. Cottagers goes to 4°F with *no* damage!

KOHLRABI
Half Hardy

B. oleracea caulorapa
Purple Vienna (Everywhere)
Vienna (Everywhere)
Danish (JSS)
Lauke (TER)

Kohlrabi, or Hungarian Turnip as it has sometimes been called, is mainly a summer crop. But if you like it, you can sow as early as the beginning of March under frames and a little later outside.

For the fall crop you can sow during the end of July and the first bit of August. Lauko is a recommended late variety; it doesn't get as woody and hot. Kohlrabi is grown for its swollen base, but the stems and leaves are good too, cooked or raw.

I don't grow kohlrabi myself. Most of this information came from Johnny's and Territorial's seed catalogs and from Dennis Scott, the Kohlrabi King of Whatcom County.

MUSTARDS   Hardy

Various forms of *Brassica chinensis, juncea,* and pekinensis; Pak Choy, Bok Choy, Green Wave, Tai Tsai, Mizuna, Tendergreen, Santoh Frilled, Price Choy, etc.

There are lots of good mustards for early spring greens. The Japanese are doing a lot of breeding work with them, so you can expect to see many new ones in the years to come. I like to sow them with the turnips under cold frames at the end of February. When I remove the frames in April I cover the small plants with some mosquito netting from a camping store (see Sharecroppers). This also shades them a bit, and they grow much leafier than they would just out in the open.

Pak-Choi

Mustards are also good for fall solar frame work in the colder climates. I don't bother with them in the fall myself, since there are the Chinese cabbages and so many other bulky brassicas. But they are very useful for small city gardens where the climate is mild. They last well down to 18°F. If you do grow them for fall use, you can start in late August and sow till October. The August sowings need to be protected from the rootfly.

RAAB/RAPA

Hardy

Brassica rapa ruvo

This is a small mustard-like brassica which you sow in late August/early September for an early spring crop. It's not terribly hardy. Nor is it very interesting to me. Italians like it though, so maybe I'm missing something.

RADISH

Hardy

Raphinus sativum
China Rose
Black Spanish
Daikon types

European radishes are well known as one of the earliest spring crops and can also be sown under frames if you are anxious to have them for the fall.

The Daikon types, which are long and often larger than carrots, can be sown in July and early August. (These sowings must be protected against rootfly maggots.) They can be stored in the ground till Thanksgiving and in mild areas till Christmas. You can also lift them and store in damp sand like carrots. I haven't tried this because I'm not fond of them.

> *Straddling over the daikon*
> *I pulled it up with all my might:*
> *Its root was small.*
>
> *Ginko*

ROCKET   Half Hardy

Eruca sativa

Rocket is a small, unselected brassica with a nutty taste reminiscent of watercress. It will grow almost anywhere. It is not especially hardy to frost but will germinate in the wettest and coldest of spring soils. It comes charging out of the ground in a couple of days (hence, I suppose, its name) and shows an admirable ability to obtain phosphorus from cold soils. Weather that makes turnip seedlings look sick is nothing to rocket. I have taken to sowing a few plants among the overwintering cold frame lettuces, and then again in mid-spring.

Below is a response from a friend who read my unenthusiastic comments about rocket in my first manuscript. It is a perfect example of the individuality of tastes and gardens.

> *(Rocket was) my first crop and absolutely delicious despite your disdain! Try it in pocket bread with hummus or in salad with feta cheese and you'll become a convert. The slugs didn't touch it, which I suppose is why it* **was** *my first crop. (It has beautiful flowers, too!)*
>
> *Judy Munger*

I must admit that by this time I have gotten rather more fond of it! Which is a good example of how your tastes can change when you have something available in the garden "off season."

RUTABAGA   Hardy

Brassica napus var. *napobrassica*
Laurentian (everywhere)
Altasweet (TER)

Though rumors are that Altasweet is the best, I can't tell much difference between the varieties. I find only a limited use for rutabagas because there are so many other winter roots I prefer.

But they are fairly hardy and can be grated raw in salads, steamed, mashed, and put in soups and stews. They are also a good crunchy surprise in Kim Chi.

SEA KALE   Very Hardy

Crambe maritima
Lily White (CHASE, BARBER)

This rather exotic and bitter crucifer grows wild on the seacoasts of Britain. Crowns of it are grown in British gardens or kept in cellars for forcing in the early spring. This produces long white stalks which are used like asparagus or chard (which is often called Sea Kale Beet). There are good descriptions of how to do this forcing in Simons and Shewell-Cooper. Sea Kale is definitely not one of your frontline staples, rather it's a luxury item. I've been too busy to try it, but if you want to you can write to England for seed.

TURNIPS   Very Hardy

B. rapa

There are three main uses for turnips: early spring sowings for roots and tops; late summer sowings for storage roots; and late summer and fall sowings for tops, or "greens."

Yorii Spring (JSS) is one of my favorites for the February sowings under frames. But there are many others listed in the catalogs which you should try if you like turnips.

The yellow varieties—Golden Ball, Orange Jelly, Golden Perfection—are the best for fall roots. They store well and are perfectly hardy if left in the ground through the winter. Southerners prefer turnip tops for the fall and overwintering crops and perfer varieties such as Crawford, Just Right, and Seven Top (HAST, PARK). There is also a new variety of turnip available from Vermont called the Gillfeather which is apparently very good tasting and vigorous (see Seed Companies; Elysian Hills).

If you are serious about your turnips, Hills has a very good section on them.

WATERCRESS   Hardy

Nasturtium officionale
Watercress (ABL, JSS)

This is found in ditches and streams of even such cold areas as the Midwest. Watercress is easy to start from either seed or cuttings. You might be able to get a bunch of it from a farmer at a local market and try rooting it in water or very moist sand. It will produce well in any place with rich soil that you can keep moist through the summer.

It is not particularly hardy, though when it grows in running water it is protected from light frosts. It crops best in the early spring and fall. It will self-sow like mad if allowed to go to seed in the summer. In fact, it is so weedy and vigorous and moves downstream at such an alarming rate that I question the wisdom of allowing it in your favorite stream. Sure is good in salads and soups though!

And that's the end of the Brassicas!

OTHER VEGETABLES

BROAD BEAN/FAVA

Vicia faba
Windsor
Windsor Long Pod

Hardy

Hills says that there are two basic varieties of fava beans: the Long Pod type, for sowing in November (Solly and Seattle Garden Center's Bob Gill say November 10 in the Seattle area) and the Windsor type for February. A March or April sowing is fine if you don't have black aphid (black fly) in your area. Black aphids can overwinter on Bigleaf maples; if you have those in your district and they are infested, you should try for a November or a January sowing so that you will have well-grown plants by the time the aphids make their appearance in the spring. Then you can just cut back the tender tops which the aphids attack.

In hard frost areas, where November and January sowings may not survive, try a February sowing and aphid patrols in infested areas (see Sharecroppers).

In hard frost areas, where November and January sowings may not survive, try a February sowing and a daily aphid patrol in infested areas (see Sharecroppers).

In either case, favas are ready before the *Phaseolus* beans (and *sometimes* before the peas). I find them best when the seeds are the size of a large thumbnail as later the skin gets tough (though the seed inside still tastes good). Some books recommend eating the pods when they are the size of small *Phaseolus* beans, but I find them bitter even when they are that small. The big dried beans are good in soups and stews but need long cooking.

BEETS   Hardy

Beta vulgaris
Lutz
Winterkeeper (STK)

Winterkeeper and Lutz are the two standard winter beets. I can't find much difference between them. Any of the small beet varieties (e.g., Detroit) will do, too.

Beets for keeping should be sown in late June or early July so they have time to mature their tender, sweet, big roots. Both Lutz and Winterkeeper have pale green leaves which taste rather like chard. If you have frosts that go much below 15°F you should mulch or else lift and store them in a cool place.

BURDOCK   Very Hardy

Arctium minus
Takinogawa (ABL, JSS)

I used to collect burdock wild in the Midwest. It is strange tasting but good. The Italians, the Japanese, and J. de B. Levy (see Winter Crops for Livestock References) place great store in its medicinal qualities.

Sow in the spring (it's a slow grower) and gather from fall onwards. However, don't let it go to seed and escape to your land; it's a pernicious weed, and if you have sheep, the burrs will make the wool unusable. Good in soups, stews, and stir fries.

CARDOONS

Half Hardy

Cynara cardunculus
(DAM, RICHTER)

Cardoons are a tall relative of globe artichokes with a similar taste. In the fall, their stalks must be blanched even higher than celery by wrapping with paper. When blanched in this way, they will stand until December. Simons, *The Oxford Book of Food Plants*, and especially Pellegrini,[2] have good descriptions of how to grow these.

Cardoons are sown in May and harvested in November. After the first harvest in the fall, you can let them overwinter for a good final crop in spring. The seeds generally don't mature this far north.

I tried growing cardoons and was rather disappointed in them. I found them fuzzy and bitter, and nothing I did seemed to remove these problems. I was not inspired to try again. If you are inspired, you had better confer with an expert. They take up a lot of space.

CARROTS

Hardy

Dauca carota

In my first garden in Seattle, I inadvertently left carrots in the ground all winter and they were great till April. Unfortunately, every other place I've gardened in the Northwest has been infested with Carrot Rust Fly maggot (see Sharecroppers), a nasty relative of the Cabbage Root Fly maggot. When these attack, they leave long, grey and rust-colored tunnels that make the carrot bitter.

So now I harvest them and store in damp sand or peat. If you don't have the fly (or wireworm) and want to store carrots in the ground, mulch them well for they are ruined by freezing lower than 10°F.

For several years I tried different varieties of carrots for summer eating and storage. One type I tried, Scarlet Keeper (JSS), kept like mad but was rather tasteless. We ended up not eating it. Then I discovered that my favorite munching carrot, Tip Top (JSS), stores admirably. I just have to time the sowings so that the storage crop is ready at the first hard frost but doesn't get overmature and split. It goes into storage at peak quality and comes out almost that way. By all means, try some of the European storage types, but if you find you don't like them as well as your favorite summer carrot, try the above technique on your favorite type.

CELERAIC   Hardy

Apium graveolens var. *rapaceum*
Blanco (JSS)
Alabaster

Celeraic is one of my favorite winter roots. It's very versatile, tasting good in soups and stews, grated fresh into salads, or steamed with a cream sauce. You can use it to replace celery stalk in recipes.

Celeraic needs to be started early in flats and kept in a frame till it's warm. Up North I start them in April in flats and put them out in June with one transplanting into pots in between. Since they need a very rich, moisture-retentive soil I put a layer of newspaper in a flat and then add two inches of fresh or composted cow manure without any bedding. Then I put in two inches of potting soil and firm it down. The seeds go on top of this and are kept fairly moist both before and after they germinate. They are quite slow growing, but when they get crowded in the flat, I put them into individual pots. By using this method I have been able to get big, mature roots by harvest time, even in hard clay soil. I store them dry or in damp sand. In milder districts like the islands or cities, they can be left in the ground. They should be mulched if frosts go much below 18°F.

Use treated seed as celeraic is susceptible to Celery Leaf Spot which is also a problem for parsley, one of the best winter greens.

CELERY Half Hardy

Apium graveolens
Utah 52-70
Leaf Celeries

In my seattle garden, most Utah celery plants overwintered without any difficulty, just a few frozen outer leaves. They tasted very strong and bitter though, being mostly good for soups and stews, but *very* good for that! A few plants lived three years, which surprised me since they are supposed to be biennial. I suppose it's because I took the center flower stalk to eat before it bloomed.

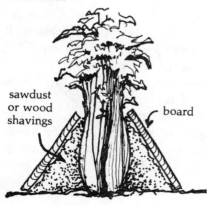

sawdust or wood shavings — board

Celery Mulch

Much below 18°F the centers die out, so if you live in a cold spot and want to carry them over, try a high mulch (or putting them in cold frames, cloches, or plastic sheds). If the outer leaves die back before you use them, be sure to take them off. Mushy, rotten stalks will eventually rot the core of the plant.

I have not had much luck with mulching regular celery

in Whatcom County. I use one of the leaf celeries instead, which are hardier. I start them along with the celeriac and then put the plants in a protected place such as a coldframe or a bed to the south of a wall. Here they are quite happy most winters and produce new leaves from the center as I pick the outer ones.

I have also tried growing the winter celeries that are available in Suttons and other English catalogs. For the life of me, I can't see why they bother with them. They have tough, bitter leaves like those of celeriac, but no swollen root. They are not as hardy as the leaf celeries, and they are much more fuss to grow. They are supposed to be for blanching by mulching in a trench. I'm afraid I find that too much work.

CHICKWEED   Very Hardy

Stellaria media
Chickweed (ABL)

A "weed" of most garden soils, chickweed makes an excellent living green mulch for Brussels sprouts and broccolis, though it rather overwhelms lettuce and onions if you have good soil. It can be a bother in the cool seasons of the year and in a rainy summer it never dies back. It is a serious weed in heavy soils. Regular and frequent cultivation is the only way to keep it under control. If by some chance you *don't* have chickweed in your garden I suggest you pick it in the fields or a friend's garden.

The size of the leaf indicates the fertility of the soil—as big as watercress, fantastic! A side effect of growing chickweed on rich soils is that the bigger leaves are more succulent and have better flavor. I clip the stems with scissors to avoid pulling the lower parts of the runners out of the dirt and use the plant in salads. J. de B. Levy says it has medicinal qualities.[3]

Dear Binda,
Did you know that
chickweed (Stellaria media)
was still a real vegetable in
medieval times? I once read
an old guild statute, where
all the different courses of a
meal were described, which
the wife of a Master Crafts-
man had to serve to the
journeymen and there was
also Mierlein or chickweed
mentioned. How times
change!

Ute Grimlund
Marysville, Washington

CHICORY   Hardy

Chicorium intybus
Root
  Witloof (French endive)
Leaf
  Red Verona (SUT, NICHOLS)
  Sugarhat (BURPEE)
  Sugarloaf (SUT)
  Greenlof (DAM)

Root chicory grows like a regular lettuce (but it's *very slow*). It is lifted in the fall (when you have time) and stored in the root cellar in a box of dry sand.

When you want some sprouts take a few roots and put them in a box or pot of wet sand. Cover them or keep in a dark place. The roots will send up shoots which will be soft, blanched, and elongated because of the darkness. When they are about 5 inches tall they can be cut off and eaten. They are slightly bitter, but have a great texture. They are wonderful in salads. Europeans cook them, and though I've never tried it, I suspect it's a mistake. I've also never taken the time to force the root chicories. I find the leaf chicories to be easier and more suited to my winter schedule.

These are sown in June in a fairly good soil and kept weeded. They should be thinned to six inches apart in the row. By late September they have formed big, smooth heads rather like a Cos (romaine) lettuce which you can harvest as you want. They keep for months in the refirgerator in a plastic bag as long as they are clean of disease and dry on the outside as they go in. They are bitter, but this decreases with storage. If you have a mild climate you could leave them out in the garden. I like them in salads mixed with other greens. They have a great texture. The red-streaked types are especially beautiful.

CORN SALAD   Very Hardy

Valerianella olitoria
Large Leaved English
Large Leaved Dutch
Vert de Cambrai (ABL, VIL)

Garden Corn Salad was derived from a weed in the "corn" (grain) fields of Europe. It is a low-growing, three-inch plant with a very soft, distinctive flavor. As it is a winter annual it germinates with the late summer or fall rains and overwinters in the rosette form. In spring it puts on a lot of growth, sending out three or four flower stalks from each plant. Although it's small, I think it is one of the better winter crops. In Holland they have whole greenhouses full of it for market.

I like it in salads from September till the end of April, but it is most useful from January through March when there is a shortage of salad material. The flowers are a forget-me-not blue and just as delicious as the rest of the plant.

If you are growing it for the first time, sow it thinly in late July, or just after the first heavy August rains. You can also make a September sowing in milder or more southern parts. I have clumps of it established in my herb beds and just let it go to seed on its own. In the summer I weed the areas where it grows once or twice, and then in the late summer the seedlings emerge where they will. It's very handy not having to worry about sowing it! If you want to save seed, spread newspapers under the plants to catch them because they ripen unevenly and drop to the ground over a month's time.

The large-leaved English types give you more winter bulk, but I really like the flavor of the smaller French one, so I grow them both. Sometimes I suspect, though, that I couldn't tell them apart in a blindfold taste test!

Corn Salad

DANDELION

Very Hardy

Taraxacum officinale

Another weed, dandelion is very good from February through Arpil. You can dig the young plants and steam them, or pick the tiny unopened flower buds and eat them raw in salads. Covering or blanching the leaves makes them into a very acceptable salad addition.

ENDIVE-ESCAROLE   Half Hardy

Chichorium endiva

Curly Endive and the flatter-leaved Escarole are good fall and early winter crops, especially under frames. I prefer the Batavian varieties as the hearts blanch well and get sweeter as the winter progresses. They are not hardy, however, and except in mild areas without much winter rain, they should be kept under glass. If you like to eat the whole head at once, rather than picking the outer leaves, you can blanch (whiten) the plants by putting a flower pot over one head at a time. The centers are usually somewhat blanched anyhow.

They should be sown in June or early July to get big heads. If you miss these sowings and are going to grow them under glass you can sow as late as August in the North.

FLORENCE FENNEL   Hardy

Foeniculum vulgare var. *dulce*
Florence Fennel (ABL)

Italian in origin and not often found for sale, Florence Fennel is worthy of more attention by local gardeners and cooks. Sown in early to mid-July, it grows somewhat like celery with a funny, swollen base. Cut off the leaves, and eat them raw in salads or steam them, or saute them in a little butter. Marvelous and succulent. The root is good, too.

I avoided Florence Fennel at first, because I'm not terribly fond of fennel seed flavor, but this almost disappears in the cooking. The plants will go through several light frosts, and last till November in the North and perhaps later in the South or milder areas.

I avoided Florence Fennel at first, because I'm not terribly fond of fennel seed flavor, but this almost disappears in the cooking. The plants will go through several light frosts, and last till November in the North and perhaps later in the South or milder areas.

Florence Fennel

GOOD KING HENRY/Mercury   Very Hardy

Chenopodium bonus henricus
Good King Henry (RDWD, RICHTER, Well Sweep)

I haven't grown or tasted this, but I'm very fond of its relative
C. album (Fat Hen, Lambs Quarters, Goosefoot), which is an
annual weed of the summer garden. Good King Henry is a perennial which shoots up very early in the spring. You eat the stalks
like asparagus or, if you wait till later, eat the leaves like spinach.
It will do well in any rich garden soil (in the perennial section, of
course).

I suggest buying a live plant (Well-Sweep) because I have
bought seed and sown it twice to no avail. It's a weed, so until
you find out more about its growth patterns, keep it restrained.

JERUSALEM ARTICHOKE   Very Hardy

Helianthus tuberosum
Stampede (JSS)

This perennial species of sunflower produces a large quantity of tubers that can be left in the ground all winter. They are very "weedy" and tall and belong well away from and to the north of, the rest of the garden. They are good raw in salads or lightly sauteed, but not boiled as they are even easier than potatoes to overcook.

Get some healthy looking tubers from a local co-op or supplier whenever they are available. They can be planted in the ground anytime you get them, from October till May, but they won't be ready for eating till the following fall. Then they can be dug as wanted from October until April. They store well in plastic bags in the refrigerator or a month or more. Mice and slugs like them, but the plants almost always produce more tubers than you can possibly eat anyhow.

LETTUCE   Hardy

Latuca sativa

Due to the general passion for lettuce, there are many different sorts, and most of them are suited to fall, winter and early spring production. It is possible to sow lettuce in any month from February until October, either in cold frames or outside. To have a continuous supply, however, you only need five or six sowings timed to your situation and microclimate. The Dutch, French, and English have done most of the work with cool season varieties, and some of the better ones come from them. But several "garden store variety" American ones such as Oakleaf and Prizehead perform well, too.

Early Spring Varieties

There are many good varieties for sowing under frames in February. I sometimes start the seedlings right in between the overwintered lettuces and early peas to save on space. Then I move some of them out in April when the frames are getting crowded and it is warm enough for them to do well. Good ones I've tried are Kwiek (SUT) (though the catalogs recommend it for fall sowing), Oakleaf, Prizehead, Buttercrunch, Little Gem (SUT) (a dwarf romaine), and May Queen (SUT). Really, this is an easy time to produce lettuce under a frame; the days are getting longer and warmer, and there is such vitality that disease is usually not a problem.

Fall Varieties

Sowings in late July and August will provide lettuces for September through December, and later under frames. These are hard ones to get going due to the summer heat and dryness. If you have a rainy break the soil should be cool enough to germinate the lettuce. Otherwise, make your sowings about 2 p.m. to 4 p.m. and water well. The seed will have the cool night to begin germination. This technique, recommended by Salter in *Know and Grow Vegetables,* is based on the particular dormancy response of lettuce seed to heat.

Good varieties are Little Gem (SUT) for winter cold frames; Winter Density (JSS), a medium-sized romaine to be covered after Thanksgiving in colder areas; Winter Marvel (Merveille d'hiver) (VIL), the best butterhead type that I have tried for overwintering, with quite a bit of rot resistance; Prizehead; and Oakleaf. Many people use Black Seeded Simpson, and English books mention Valdor, Imperial Winter and Arctic King a lot.

Whichever variety does well for you, keep it well spaced (9 inches on center) and dust the soil with basalt, volcanic ash, or sulfur to prevent disease. I find that in the North I have to cover this set of lettuce by November if I want it to last through the winter. More often, because of the rot problem, I just let it freeze and go without lettuce until the October-sown varieties under glass start to produce in March. I guess I enjoy having a break from lettuce. I focus instead on grated carrots, corn salad and sprouts for my salads. If *you* prefer lettuce at this time and live in an area with frequent hard freezes, you will want to have some rugs or mats to put over your frames when the temperatures drop.

Overwintering Varieties

If you were away in August or were too busy to sow fall lettuce, you can still do a sowing under frames in September and October that will overwinter and begin to produce extra leaves by early March and whole heads by the middle of April. I find this batch very useful as I begin to enjoy lettuce again just about this time. Good varieties, listed in order of cropping, are Kwiek, Winter Marvel, Prizehead, and Little Gem. It's very interesting to watch these little lettuce seedlings slowly come up to size through the winter and then in February and March race away to form heads.

NEW ZEALAND SPINACH   Hardy?

Tetragonia expansa

I don't grow New Zealand Spinach as I'm not fond of it, but those who do tell me that it is as cold hardy as it is heat resistant. Apparently in a mild fall you can have it till Christmas.

ONIONS

Onions are such a wonderful and staple vegetable that it's comforting to know that you can have them all year round—green or bulb, as you prefer.

SCALLION/Welsh Onion   Very Hardy

Allium fistulosum

Scallions are a nonbulbing perennial. In their original form they grow in clumps with small, slightly swollen bottoms (not real bulbs), and multiply like chives. In this form they were for centuries the common garden onion of China and Japan. They flower in midsummer and then die down. With the September/October rains, they start growing and are usable again. Growth slows down around the solstice if it's a cold winter, but basically they are available till June or sometimes July in a rainy spring. Their flowers, which come on in June, are good for salads. There are several commercial permutations of the scallion emphasizing different traits. Some are nonhardy, but Evergreen Hardy White, Hardy White Bunching, He Shiko, and Kujo Multistalk make it through even New England winters (JSS, ABL, TER). Beltsville Bunching and Sweet Spanish, sold as scallions, are actually *A. cepa* and are not as hardy. To start off a scallion patch sow seed anytime in the spring or early summer. Fall plantings can be made, too.

OVERWINTERING ONIONS   Very Hardy

A. cepa
Sweet Winter (TER)
OW171 (JSS)

These handy types are sown in the very end of July or the first week of August in a seed bed. Once they are large enough (end of September usually), you can put them out at a normal spacing to overwinter. You can pull them as green onions from about April on. They begin to bulb up in May and are usually ready for harvest as dried bulbs by mid- to late June. It is important to observe the correct sowing date so that they are large enough to make it through the winter, but not so large that they bolt the following spring. These are not super keepers, but they will last until your regular bulb onions are ready.

TOP SET ONIONS   Very Hardy

A. cepa proliferum
Egyptian/Tree onions/Multipliers (ABL)

Although these onions are very hardy and good tasting I have given up growing them. I didn't find them very prolific compared to the hardy scallions. You can propagate them two ways:

1) By topsets, or bulblets (little bulbs that form at the top of the stalk where the flower should be, or sometimes in coexistence with them). These you can harvest in midsummer when they are ripe and plant for greens in the fall. They will then turn into next year's mature onions. The stalks will die down, leaving the big bulbs in the soil.

Top Onion

2) Harvest three or four of the big bulbs, leaving one in place to multiply. Or harvest them all and select out the best to replant for reproduction. These bulbs are strong flavored, and at their best when dug from the soil in mid-winter.

Once you have these growing in your garden, you should have them for a long time as they are very persistent, "very hardy," and don't require much attention, not even weeding. I had top onions in Wisconsin under an old apple tree, and they propagated themselves happily there, year after year, going through minus thirty degree freezes and three feet of snow.

Miscellaneous Onion Family
Greens for Winter   Very Hardy

If you are in a hurry and haven't got starts of any of the other types you can plant onion sets, garlic cloves, or shallots for a supply of greens through the winter. They can be planted anytime from early September through October, and pulled as greens when desired.

LEEKS   Very Hardy

Allium ampeloprasum var. *porrum*

I have come to treasure leeks in the last few years. They are so hardy, so tasty, so attractive, and in our area, not bothered by much. They fill the gap if you run out of bulb onions. They also have a unique flavor and are good in soups, baked, pickled, etc.

They are slow-growing, and like onions, delicate and small for the first two months. So it is a good idea to start them in seed beds or flats in April. In June lift them, trim the tops and roots, and plant them at 6- to 8-inch spacing. I can get three or four rows in my 36-inch beds. This gives me a slightly smaller leek, but I prefer them that way.

Fall Varieties   ⁝S

Elephant, Blue de Solaise, Inverno, and other faster growing leeks are not so hardy. They tend to have paler green leaves and start to slime up by late November, but they are good till then.

Winter Varieties

Alaska (STK)
Giant Winter (SUT)
Carentan (DAM)
Winta (TER)
Musselberg

These are stockier, with dark, blue-green leaves, and the better sorts stand the worst weather that the maritime climate can dish out. In exceedingly bad years they get some core damage, but will often regrow by April. My all-time favorite is Carentan. It's the hardiest I've grown, having had an 80 percent survival rate in the fierce winter of 1978-1979, and it has a nice flavor. Carentan never grows very large (some leeks get monstrous and, to my mind, are not worth eating) and is always tender enough for salads. It also has no bulge at the base of the shaft, and hence, is easier to lift from the soil and to clean. But most years I try new leeks just to compare them, and who knows, maybe some day I'll find something to supercede Carentan.

PARSLEY   Very Hardy

Petroselium crispum

I find parsley too strong in the heat of summer, but by fall it has sweetened up with the rains and cool nights. The only trouble is that most American varieties are bred for tenderness and won't stand up to cold weather. The best I've tried are the European varieties from Stokes—Bravour and Darki—which do well all winter, and Delikat (JSS), which, though it has not been as productive for me in the winter months, has not bolted so soon in the spring. Green Velvet (TER) sounds like it might fit both summer *and* winter uses.

I am very fond of plain, or Italian, parsley. In my garden it has been hardier than American curled sorts though it isn't much better than the three mentioned above. I believe if you have a strain of plain parsley you like you could select for winter hardiness and end up with a good thing.

Sowing dates for winter cropping are the same as those for summer use. You can also sow later in June, but you will get smaller plants.

PARSNIP   Very Hardy

Pastinaca sativa
Any variety

Parsnips were the potatoes of Europe before Columbus and all that. Today they are in disregard but, in fact, have many uses. They are delicious grated in stir fries, soups, stews, cakes, baked, and just plain steamed. They are very hardy, though vulnerable in heavy, wet soil, where they get a form of rot called canker. If your parsnips show signs of this, make raised beds, sow them later or closer to get smaller roots, and use resistant varieties such as Avonresister and White Gem (SUT).

In the North they can be sown in April or May, and in the South until June or July if you want very small ones. Make sure to keep them well weeded. A mulch helps if you have a fine enough material. As a root crop they should go on soil that was well dug and manured for a previous crop.

PEAS   Not Hardy

Pisum sastivum

It is theoretically possible to do a July sowing of peas and get a fall crop just before the fall frosts. The problems are that it is hard to keep these moisture and cool loving plants going through the rigors of the hottest part of the summer. Even if you do manage this, there is a virus disease in the Northwest called pea enation that will cripple most varieties. There are a few resistant types being released. I've tried some of them, and so far I'd say it's not worth the trouble, if you live in a pea growing area where the disease is heavy. But if you live in an out-of-the-way corner and there isn't any disease or much of it, and you *love* peas, you might try them. Territorial and Nichols have both carried resistant varieties. Also check with your local extension agent.

SALSIFY

Tragopogon porrifolius

Very Hardy

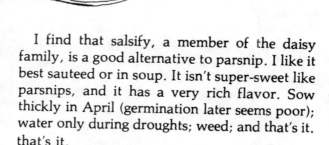

I find that salsify, a member of the daisy family, is a good alternative to parsnip. I like it best sauteed or in soup. It isn't super-sweet like parsnips, and it has a very rich flavor. Sow thickly in April (germination later seems poor); water only during droughts; weed; and that's it. that's it.

In the spring the new leaves are good cooked or as a salad green. Salsify is biennial, so if you want to save your own seed, just leave one plant and it will shoot up to 4-5 feet in May and show its purple flowers through June mornings. The seeds come in a ball like dandelions (and are just as weedy), so catch them before they shatter in a wind on dry July days.

SCORZONERA

Scorzonera hispanica

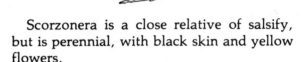

Scorzonera is a close relative of salsify, but is perennial, with black skin and yellow flowers.

The difference between them is subtle, and I'm not sure I could tell them apart blindfolded. However, scorzonera does have straighter, longer roots and, in my experience makes a heavier crop. You can leave it two years in the ground; the roots just get bigger.

The cultural requirements are the same as with salsify, but I think deep digging would really be merited here. The roots can be up to 18 inches long, so unless your soil is very loose, you will often lose the bottom part when you dig the plant. On the other hand, if you don't have the time, strength, or weather to dig a bed in April, don't worry. The roots will get down into the subsoil by themselves, drawing up valuable nutrients for you to eat in January and February.

If you have plantain growing in your garden, it will be hard to distinguish the two in the seedling stage. The differences are that scorzonera leaves have serrated edges and a downiness on the inner surfaces.

SKIRRET

Hardy?

Sium sisarum
(WELL, SSE)

I *still* haven't tried this vegetable, but many reports say it's worth it. A member of the Seed Savers Exchange sent me an enthusiastic note about it.

Apparently it's best started from root divisions, but it will come from seed if you get it fresh. It's a member of the carrot family, and the German name, Zuckerwurzel, seems to imply some sweetness.

Reports are that you can store the roots in the ground over winter, or in sand like carrots.

SPINACH

Very Hardy

Spinacea oleracea
Cold Resistant Savoy (STK)
Giant Winter (ABL, DAM)
Winter Bloomsdale
Sigmaleaf (SUT)
Dixi Market (HAST)

Spinach is amazingly hardy, but you have to give it a decent soil and a well-drained bed to over-winter in. If sown in late July/early August it will give you a fine fall crop as well as plenty of leaves till about Christmas. Then it rests till March (February in a mild winter) and comes on again. In cold sites it's best to cover it with glass from mid-December till the end of February if you want good production. In an early winter you could cover it by late October. In Northeaster country, a rug thrown over the frames will give added protection when the temperatures go below 15°F.

I find the savoyed (crinkly leaved) types to be sweeter, but not as productive, as the flat-leaved sorts. So if you have a large family or go in for bulk, try Giant Winter, Sigmaleaf, or similar sorts for cooking. Munsterlander, a German flat-leaved variety that I got through the Seed Savers Exchange, is an extremely productive and fairly sweet winter type. Winter Bloomsdale and Cold Resistant Savoy should be saved for salads.

Spinach germinates well in cold soil, so try to sow in a rainy break. If none is forthcoming, sow in the afternoon and keep well misted as with lettuce. In very hot summers the July sowings might bolt, especially if your soil is not moisture retentive. Then you can sow again, and though you will get smaller plants, you will still have some of this valuable winter crop. Sowings later than August are mainly good for overwintering under glass (or uncovered if in a mild district) to give you an extra early spring crop. My overwintered spinach always tastes better, looks better, has more bulk and bolts later than the early spring sowings. Though this year I threw some "old" spinach seed out with the crimson clover seed for green manure and got the best spring crop ever . . . food for thought!

SWISS CHARD   Very Hardy

Beta vulgaris var. *cicla*
Fordhook Giant (JSS)
Lucullus (ABL)
Geneva (Parks)

This is one of the few vegetables that you can regularly see overwintering in gardens around the Northwest. It is very popular in Europe where it is a big commercial crop. (In English catalogs you will find listings of Sea Kale Beet, or Spinach Beet, which are similar to Swiss chard but often don't have as big a midrib.)

If you are only growing chard for winter use, then sow it in July. I haven't grown it in years, so below are some comments on chard by my neighbor and editor, Lane Morgan, who lives in Sumas. She gardens an eighth of a mile from the Canadian border and gets full benefit of the devastating Northeasters that roar out of the Canadian mountains several times each year.

"I like it for its winter bulk and early spring rebound. The ribs aren't good past fall, but the leaves taste nice. Mine dies back in Northeasters and I cut it down to a nub so it won't rot. It starts growing again in February and lasts till May. Chard Lasagna is great. Ruby Chard is very beautiful but I have never had any luck with it. [I found it bitter myself.]

I grow Fordhook Giant. Germination is slow and the plants are initially pokey [maybe more lime?], but after they get going they are indestructible."

Cottagers Kale

HERBS

I'm putting herbs in a section of their own because, being more powerful, they aren't used in the same large quantities as the other vegetables, and it's that little bit that makes the difference, especially to your winter and spring salads, sauces, and soups. Because they haven't been bred to be all soft and puffed up the way we like the rest of our vegetables, they have more vitamins and minerals in their leaves.

Also, though many perennial herbs die back somewhat in the depth of our winters, they stay late and come back early. Their earliness is especially welcome for meals served in the doldrums of March and April. You can disguise cabbage with a lemon-thyme sauce, or revolutionize the same old salad with new lovage sprouts. Most of the herbs mentioned below are known for their medicinal properties as well as their culinary virtues, so that's another good reason to have them available for winter consumption.

CHERVIL

Hardy

Anthriscus cerefolium

I really like this small licorice-tasting plant. Chervil gives a surprising taste to winter salads, and it's no bother as it self-sows in late summer. To start it off, sow the seeds in good soil in late July/ August, and water till the plants are established. If your soil has a lot of winter weed seed in it

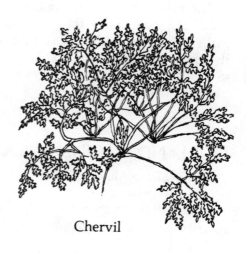

Chervil

(chickweed, groundsel, mallow, etc.), you may have trouble growing chervil. I've found it to be noncompetitive.

CHINESE LEEK/Garlic Chives   Hardy

Allium tuberosum
(JSS, WELL, RICHTER)

Known as Gow Choy by the Chinese, this tastes somewhat like garlic. It is relatively new to occidental gardeners, and is a perennial which is started from seed. It is very slow growing and not really usable until the second year. The onion-like flower stalks that appear in late summer are very attractive and good in salads. The leaves are available till late in the fall, much later than chives, but they don't come up as soon in the spring.

CHIVES   Very Hardy

Allium schoenprasum

Chives tend to die down in October or November, especially if it's a dry year. Then they reappear in late February (or even earlier if you lift and force some in a sunny window), so I think they're worth having. The lavender flowers are excellent in salads. Get a root division from a friend or buy as a bedding plant in spring.

CORIANDER/Cilantro/Chinese Parsley   Hardy

Coriandrum sativum

This herb is remarkably hardy. March sowings germinate with alacrity, and late August or early September ones will last until

January and sometimes until spring in a mild winter. The strongly aromatic leaves can be used like parsley in salads and are common in Mexican, Chinese and Indian cooking. The flowers are good in salads and an important food for syrphid flies, a predator you might want to encourage in your garden.

FENNEL   Very Hardy

Foeniculum vulgare
Seed or root division

A perennial that is around for most of the year. It dies in October/November and then comes back up early in March. Not everyone will like its strong anise-like flavor, but if you do, it's there waiting for you. I have seen quite a few wild plants in different parts of Seattle. They get very large (3 feet in diameter and 4 to 5 feet high), so be sure to put fennel where it won't interfere with your other herbs. It's a very assertive, hard-to-get-rid-of plant, so use caution.

GARLIC   Hardy/Very Hardy

Allium sativum
Silverskin, Red Spanish

If you put garlic cloves in around October, they will put up green shoots just like onions. These are milder than the cloves, and go well in salads, sauces, omelets, etc. Separate the ones for cutting from your main garlic crop, however, as cutting robs the new cloves which are forming. The larger Red Spanish variety is more vigorous through the winter. It sends up a seed stalk in the early summer.

HORSERADISH   Very Hardy

Armoracia rusticana

You can dig the root of this crucifer all winter, if you
remember to. In the spring, the pungent new leaves are a treat in
salads. It's very easy to grow from a piece of root crown; in fact,
it's hard to kill, so be sure to put it where it won't take over the
rest of your perennial herbs.

LOVAGE   Very Hardy

Levisticum officionale

This member of the carrot/celery family is a perennial and has
a wonderful unique taste. It makes an early spring or fall salad,
soup, or sauce into something special. I got my plant by root
division from a German winter gardener, but it apparently comes
easily from seed. Try to get seed fresh in that year; it ripens in
July/August. The University of Washington Herb & Drug Plant
Garden has a nice bunch of plants.

OREGANO   Variable

Origanum spp.

The pink flowered oregano, though tough and very hardy,
doesn't have much flavor. The white flowered Wild Oregano,
Origanum vulgare, has proved hardy in my garden, but the seed
is hard to find. Check Richter and Wellsweep for Greek Oregano.
While this is not too hardy it is truly super strong!

ROSEMARY   Hardy
Rosmarinus officionalis
From cuttings

Best to get a start of this, put it in a fairly dry place, and water well till it's established. Rosemary is wonderful in winter stews, and small hints of it in salads are good. It also makes a soothing tea after a long excursion in the rain.

SAGE   Very Hardy
Salvia officionalis

Most Americans know this in its dried form. It grows easily and you can have it fresh all winter, too.

SALAD BURNET   Very Hardy
Sanguisorba minor
Sometimes as: *Poterium sanguisorba*
Salad Burnet (ABL)

I feel that this is an herb of borderline usefulness. It certainly stays green throughout the winter, and it does taste of cucumbers, but rather bitter ones unfortunately. It isn't very succulent, but it does offer a nice variation in your winter salads, and it's supposed to be very good for you. To start it off, sow in spring or summer. Cows supposedly relish it.

SHUNGIKU/Garland Chrysanthemum   Hardy

Chrysanthemum coronarium

Small amounts of this are good in stir fries. For a fall into winter crop, sow in late August or early September. Sow fairly thickly and thin for use. I put a little in with the spinach or lettuce under frames.

SORREL   Very Hardy

Rumex acetosa
French Sorrel (JSS, RICHT)
R. scutatus
Plain Sorrel (ABL)
Grande de Belleville (DEM)

Plain

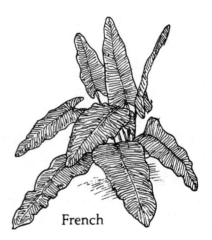

French

The sorrels impart a wonderful sour flavor to salads, but you pay for it with oxalic acid. I guess a certain amount of this doesn't hurt you, and if you aren't into lemons they are nice plants to have.

I had a German roommate in high school who said her family made a soup of sorrel during World War II called sauerumfe (or something like that). Sounds fun.

THYME
Very Hardy

Thymus vulgaris
German Winter Thyme
Lemon Thyme
Caraway Thyme
Etc.
(WELLSWEEP)

Common thyme is easily found in many gardens, so you should be able to get a start. Lemon variegated thyme, which is so good in winter salads, is less common and you might have to search a little harder for it. It isn't as hardy in its first two years and might need mulching lightly in a cold site. Caraway thyme is farily hardy and good in salads and herb butters. German winter thyme is a plain thyme that stays greener in the winter.

VIOLETS
Hardy/Very Hardy

Viola spp.

(STK, WELL, PARK, RICHT)

Wild violet flowers and leaves are edible and high in vitamin C. Swiss and Winter Flowering pansies *(Viola hyemalis)* bloom early and late and make nice additions to salads. I don't know if Sweet violet *(V. odorata)* leaves are edible, but the flowers are and have this amazing Victorian-style perfume! All the violets make a visual treat in the herb border.

WINTER SAVORY
Hardy

Satureia montana

With me this has been a short-lived perennial of variable hardiness. It tastes rather like thyme but is not as attractive or vigorous. I had better luck with it in Seattle than further north.

1. Fermentation in sauerkraut is caused by anaerobic lactic acid forming bacteria, hence the salt is really unnecessary. Daily ingestion, like when you eat yogurt, keeps your gut fauna in good shape. "Saltless" kraut is made by finely shredding fresh clean cabbage leaves and packing them with occasional spices or flavorings such as cumin or seaweed, and only enough salt to taste, rarely more than a tablespoon per gallon. Add water to cover and hold the cabbage down with a large, whole leaf or cheesecloth and a weight such as a clean stone. Place the jar in a warm spot such as one used to raise bread dough. Place a large plate beneath the jar to collect the overspill of fermentation. Poke a chopstick into the kraut several times to release air bubbles. Three or four days are needed to complete the process, after which the top particles may be cleaned off and the jar capped and stored in the refrigerator.

   Kim Chi, the Korean version of sauerkraut, is made by the same process with Chinese cabbage, leeks, red peppers such as Hungarian Hot Wax or Karlo, and fish sauce (obtainable from Asian food stores). You can also add chunky bits such as rutabagas, turnips, and other winter roots. (The Koreans make a summer Kim Chi out of cucumbers which is excellent.)

2. *The Food-Lover's Garden.* Angelo Pellegrini. 1975 reprint. Madrona Publishers, Seattle.

   Discursive, interesting book by excellent Seattle gardener, with general cultural information, recipes, etc. Discusses rocket and chicory as well as cardoons.

3. *Common Herbs for Natural Health.* J. de Bairacli Levy. p. 46.

Which Vegetables and Herbs to Grow References

Cole Crops: Botany, Cultivation & Utilization. M. Nieuwhof. 1969. Leonard Hill Co., London, England. Available from CRC Press, Inc., 2255 Palm Beach Lakes Blvd., West Palm Beach, FL 33409.

   Very "textbooky," but some revealing information on the more common of the coles. Good if you have to write a term paper and need a reference. Lots of data from studies on cold, pests, manuring, etc.

Oxford Book of Food Plants. Harrison, Masefield and Wallis. 1969. Oxford University Press, Ely House, London W1, England.

   Good reference, gorgeous illustrations.

The Vegetable Book: An Unnatural History. Yann Lovelock. 1972. St. Martins Press, New York.

   Strange and amusing poems and descriptions of common and uncommon vegetables. Library reading.

Vegetable Crops. Thompson & Kelly. McGraw Hill, Novato, CA.

   The college textbook on vegies, from Cornell. In its umpteenth edition.

Wild Flowers of Britain & Northern Europe. Fitter and Belamey. 1974. Scribner & Sons, New York.

What if You Don't Garden in the Maritime Northwest?

INTRODUCTION

Some areas of North America which lack a true maritime climate still have mild enough winters to grow crops through most of the year. In Florida, the Gulf coasts, and southern California, year-round cropping is well established. In other areas, such as northern California and the Atlantic Coast, many gardeners are not aware of the possibilities of overwintering and winter production. If you live in one of these areas, this section will acquaint you with *some* of the possibilities available to you.

If you live in eastern Washington or Oregon you will, of course, be facing a winter similar to that of the Northeast and would do well to read some of the books recommended in that section.

California

The northernmost part of California, especially along the coast, is really Maritime Northwest in climate. Although the timing may be a little advanced from southern Oregon, you are still following a basic maritime pattern of cool summers and moist, mild winters. Inland, the mountains and river valleys of the Klamath, like the Rogue, lead to such topographical complexities that it is useless for me to generalize.

Further south, in the Mendocino area, there is a good local book available to guide you. It is called *The Prosperous Gardener* by James Jankowiak, and it covers year-round gardening for that area. The Integral Urban House is an excellent source of information for the Berkeley area, and the Farallones Institute Rural Center in Occidental is also available to help you with questions. S.L.U.G. (see California Groups) is also a good source.

Informants tell me that the limiting factor for crops in the lowlands of northern California is not low temperatures so much as pests and diseases. As these are less prevalent during the winter, it is a good time to focus on the more vulnerable plants. Useful books for this area include *California Vegetable Growing, How to Grow More Vegetables, The Self-Sufficient Gardener,* and *The Complete Book of Edible Landscaping.* But the very best, I think, is the *City People's Book of Raising Food* by the Olkowskis. They are the people who helped start the Integral Urban House and their book is well worth reading. It is a model of intelligent thought and action as well as good gardening experience.

Ecology Action of the Midpeninsula has developed designs for a "multi-use mini house." This is a coldframe-like structure which can be used during the summer months to shade and protect from pests those cool season plants that need to be started during the summer.

I have not been able to find out too much about winter cropping in the coastal ranges and the foothills and higher elevations of the Sierras. I imagine that they are rather like the Alps, the Apennines and the Pyrenees, in other words, an elevated Mediterranean climate. One would do well to look toward Swiss, Spanish and Italian seed sources. Gardeners from those areas might have useful information. This is, of course, true for the coastal lowlands also.

California References

The Complete Book of Edible Landscaping. Rosaline Creasy. 1982. The Sierra Club.

The City Peoples Book of Raising Food. Helga and William Olkowski. 1975. Rodale Press, Emmaus, PA 18049.

How to Grow More Vegetables. John Jeavons. 1979. Ten Speed Press, P.O. Box 7123, Berkeley, CA 94707.

The New Western Garden Book. 1979. Sunset, Lane Publishing Co., Menlo Park, California.

The Prosperous Gardener: A Guide to Gardening the Organic Way. James Jankowiak. 1978. Rodale Press, Emmaus, PA 18049.

You'd never know from the title that this is such a *local* book, focused on coastal northern California. (I guess Rodale didn't want to advertise it as such; might cut sales.) But as far as I can see, it would be useless to a gardener in Connecticut or Colorado. Very pertinent for its area though and well worth reading.

CALIFORNIA GROUPS

Integral Urban House
1516 5th St.
Berkeley, CA 94710
Contact Rob Goodman

Ecology Action of the Midpeninsula
2225 El Camino Real
Palo Alto, CA 94360

Farallones Institute Rural Center
15290 Coleman Valley Rd.
Occidental, CA 95465

S.L.U.G. (the San Francisco League
of Urban Gardeners)
Attn. Pam Pierce
288 9th St., #6
San Francisco, CA 94103

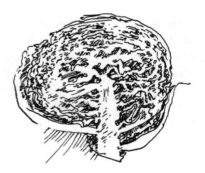

Planting Times for Coastal Bay Area

Artichoke	August-December*** or plant seed in February	Leek	February-April
Asparagus	January-February***	Lettuce (leaf)	December-August or later
Beans—snap	May-July	Lettuce (cos)	March-April
Beans—fava	November, February-April	Mustard	February-March July-August
Beets	February-August	Onions	January-March***
Broccoli	February-March June-September*	Parsley	December-May
Br. Sprouts	April-July	Parsnips	May-June or February or fall
Cabbage	January-October*	Peas	January-August November
Ch. Cabbage	July-August	Peppers	May**
Carrots	January-August	Potatoes (white)	January-August***
Cauliflower	January August-September	Pumpkins	May-June
Celeriac	March-June	Radish	All year
Celery	February-May August-September	Rhubarb	December-January
Chard	February-May	Rutabaga	July
Chayote	January-March***	Spinach	August-March
Chives	February-Arpil	Squash (summer)	May-July
Corn (sweet)	April-July 15	Squash (winter)	May-June
Cucumbers	May 1-July 15	Sunchokes	January-March***
Eggplant	May**	Sunflower	April-July 15
Endive	March-July	Tomatoes	April-May**
Garlic	October 15-February***	Turnips	January-February August
Kale	January/February or September/October		
Kohlrabi	July-August		

*Plants only after August 1
**Plants
***Root, set or other non-seed start often used

This chart was developed by Pam Pierce, president of SLUG. She has been an active community garden organizer in the Bay Area for eight years.

The Northeast

Although New England cannot be said to have mild winters, quite a lot of experience has recently been gathered there by gardeners growing crops in cold frames and solar greenhouses. In 1977 the Nearings brought out their *Sun-Heated Greenhouse* book, which described their experiences in overwintering leeks, lettuce, endive, chard and parsley in Maine. A 1981 book from Stephen Greene Press, *Intensive Gardening Round the Year*, is an extensive coverage of gardening techniques including an excellent chapter on cold season gardening under various frames. Most of the information comes from the authors' experiences in New Hampshire and Vermont.

In Ashland, Massachusetts, the Community Organic Gardening Project has been experimenting with the solar pod design developed by Solar Survival of New Hampshire. They have successfully overwintered greens and a few roots. The Coolidge Center for the Advancement of Agriculture in Topsfield, Massachusetts, is experimenting on a commercial scale and has been doing work on extending the season with Dutch Lights.

Last but not least, the Rodale group in Pennsylvania have experimented with overwintering greens in the solar cold frames (usually well reported in "Organic Gardening" magazine) and have several publications of interest to the year-round gardener in colder climates.

All of these sources supply reading lists and information on relevant seed companies.

Northeast References

Building and Using Our Sun-Heated Greenhouse. Helen and Scott Nearing. 1977. Garden Way Publishing, Charlotte, VT 05445.
  Very good book for areas with severe climate or cold spells. Simple, straightforward descriptions with lots of photos of cool season crops.

The Food and Heat-Producing Solar Greenhouse, by W. Yanda and R. Fisher, 1980, J. Muir Publications, Santa Fe, NM.

Intensive Gardening Round the Year. Paul Doscher, Timothy Fisher and Kathleen Kolb. 1981. Stephen Greene Press, Brattleboro, VT 05301.

Really useful book for would-be year-round gardeners in continental climates.

The Solar Greenhouse Book. James C. McCullagh. 1978. Rodale Press, Emmaus, PA.

I'm not yet into greenhouses, but it looks like a useful book if I were!

Solar Survival Press, Box 119, Harrisville, NH 03450.

Sells a reprint of a 1913 book, *Intensive Culture of Vegetables, French System,* and plans for solar pods, cones, etc.

"Summary of Cool-Weather Crops Tested 1979-80 for Solar Structures." Eileen Weinsteiger. 1981. Horticulture Dept., Organic Gardening and Farming Research Center. Rodale Press, Emmaus, PA.

If you like to grow greens and salad crops under frames, read this.

NORTHEAST GROUPS

Coolidge Center for the Advancement of Agriculture, Riverhill Farm, Topsfield, MA 01983.

Community Organic Gardening Project, Parish Hall, Esty St., Ashland, MA 01721.

Organic Gardening and Farming Research Center, RD1, Kutztown, PA 19530.

Owned and operated by Rodale Press (which has a reader service with a current list of local organic gardening and farming groups). You can ask them for copies of their numerous articles and research papers on cool weather crops and solar structures.

Southeast

Many areas in the Southeast are suitable for winter crops. In fact, some vegetables, such as spinach, collards, and kale, are grown there in the winter by commercial truck farmers.

There are two main impediments to regular and reliable winter cropping. One is the heat of the summer, which encourages insect pests and inhibits the growing of many of the heat-sensitive maritime vegetables. The other is that storms from the coldest parts of the continent often bring sudden, severe winter weather even to the coastal strip. Both of these problems can be dealt with, but it takes a bit of extra time and energy and probably limits crops and varieties to those which can be most easily protected.

Late sowing, shading, and screening are probably the most effective defenses against summer heat and insects. A large modular structure which can be fitted over beds would probably serve well; the design developed by Ecology Action of the Midpeninsula might be useful (see California section). When cold weather threatens, the screening can be replaced by glass or fiberglass panels, and during very severe cold spells, matting or rugs can be placed over the frames to further insulate them.

The best crops for this intensive frame culture are the cut-and-come-again greens such as spinach, green onions, dwarf kales, herbs, lettuce and endive, and the Asian brassicas. I have spoken to gardeners from the Southeast coast and the Appalachians who have successfully carried over these crops, so if you are interested in fresh greens for much of the winter you could try too!

Southeast References

Carolina Farm Stewardship Association
  Attn: Debbie Wechsler
  Graham Center
  Rt. 3, Box 05
  Wadesboro, NC 28170
  Emphasis on commercial production.

Carolina Center for Biological Husbandry
  Attn: R. Otto
  Earth Studies Department
  Appalachian State
  Boone, NC 28608
  Emphasis on research for subsistence farmers.

Virginia Association of Biological Farmers
  Attn: Earl Lawrence
  Rt. 3, Box 213
  Rocky Mount, VA 24151

Piedmont Organic Growers
  Attn: Elizabeth Crippen
  Rt. 2, Mt. View Rd.
  Taylors, SC 29687

Winter Crops
for
Livestock

INTRODUCTION

When I undertook the care of animals I was excited to find that there were as many foods available to them in the winter as there were to me. I discovered that hay, grain, and poor winter pasture were not the only possibilities for livestock. After doing some reading and after observing chickens, ducks, sheep, and goats through the winter, I began to understand that just as my diet had been restricted by the dictates of the supermarket, so had theirs by the local feed store and the recommendations of those who sell pasture mixtures.

I believe that the physical well-being of your livestock is certainly as important as your own, whether you keep a few rabbits and chickens in your backyard, or a flock of sheep, goats, or a cow on pasture. You have a special responsibility to provide for your animals. They are restrained from wandering at will and selecting from a wide range of vegetation what they need to meet the nutritional requirements of their yearly cycle.

Basically, as I see it, the problem is one of habitat. Most of your livestock originated in Eurasia, and throughout their evolution fed on the vegetation of that area. The native vegetation of the Maritime Northwest is *not* similar to that of mid-Europe. Our vegetation is mainly coniferous and in many places it lacks crucial elements for stock, such as abundant meadowlands, shrubbery and extensive deciduous woodlands, all diverse in plant and animal species.

When pastures were established in the Maritime Northwest, they were unavoidably created from· mixtures bought at the store. What's more, these pastures were being established during the rise of modern "scientific" agriculture, so the seed mixtures were monotypic, lacking in important forage plants, many of which would have been available throughout the winter.

What can you do to reverse this unhealthy trend for your stock? You can study the lists in this section and the books I have recommended and increase the diversity of the natural feed available for your animals. Not only will your animals be healthier, but in the end this approach could probably lower your feed costs a small amount since most of the feed sources I have listed are perennial plants.

I have divided the available winter feed into three categories: succulents (such as kale); pasture plants (herbs, legumes and grasses); and browse (hedgerow plants with their buds, catkins, bark, fruit and nuts). There is also hay, (out of the realm of this book), and what McKenzie calls concentrates which deserves some comment.

Concentrates are condensed proteins and carbohydrates, available in such foods as milk powders, grains, soybeans, linseed cake, and other by-products of industry. They are very rich and I feel not all that suitable in the diets of animals except in small amounts or at particular stress points through the year. Browse, in fact, is a natural form of concentrates. Allowing your animals to eat from hedgerows gives them access to nutrients that various perennial plants produce.

Succulents

Succulents include all the leavings of your garden, and specially planted stock foods such as Marrowstem and Thousand-Headed kale, mangels (stock beets), sugar beets, turnips, rutabagas and carrots. The roots are mostly suitable for ruminants (and pigs somewhat), but the leavings of your garden and the kales are liked by poultry, rabbits and pigs as well. Succulents can provide a source of fresh vegetable feed for your animals throughout the winter.

Pasture

If you are raising livestock on an average Northwest pasture you will want to renovate it as soon as you have money and time. When you do this, you can simply include as many herb seeds as you can gather up to place with the grasses and clover you choose.

These herbs greatly increase the value of forage and hay

available to your stock during the most stressful times of the year—summer drought, winter, early spring. Many herbs are deep rooted and collect minerals that grasses and clovers do not, reducing the need for mineral supplements. They are a real asset and are well worth the extra expense of the seed and the extra effort required to seek them out.

The three best authorities that I know on the subject of herbs and pastures are David McKenzie, *Goat Husbandry*, Newman Turner, *Fertility Pastures*; and J. de Bairacli Levy, *Herbal Handbook for Farm and Stable*. The Levy and Turner books give lists of plants especially beneficial to different stock. Turner deals mostly with common herbs ("weeds") and their role in pastures. Levy deals with the more medicinal plants for hedgerows and pastures.

This is what McKenzie has to say on the importance of herbs in pastures:

> *For centuries we have been feeding our sheep and cattle on a mixture of grass, legumes, and miscellaneous fodder plants, including weeds such as daisy, buttercup and nettle, acceptable meadow species like plantain and yarrow, and cultivated pasture plants like chicory and burnet. During all of that time every farmer who wasn't stone blind knew his stock ate most of them and liked them. Until relatively recently he maintained these species on his fields by sowing out with barn sweepings. Since the introduction of pedigree seeds' mixtures, the average annual hay crop has shown no significant increase, the sale of mineral mixtures for stock-feeding has risen from near zero to over 40,000 tons per annum, and mineral deficiency disease has become a major farm problem. The effect of replacing these miscellaneous pasture plants by grass and clover is to reduce the mineral content of the sward by approximately 20 per cent.*

*No special inspiration or insight into the Work-
ings of Nature is needed to reach these conclu-
sions. Brynmor Thomas and fellow research
workers at the Durham University School of
Agriculture have investigated accurately the
earlier suggestions of R. H. Elliott and Stapledon.
Here are the facts concerning one of their trial
fields at Cockle Park.*

The Percentage Composition of the Herbage from Swards Containing Varying Percentages of Other Fodder Plants

Constituent	Standard Grass and Clover Mixture	With 10% Other Fodder Plants	With 50% Other Fodder Plants	With 100% Other Fodder Plants
Crude protein	16.75	17.19	16.90	16.94
Crude fibre	21.32	19.49	18.61	15.16
Total ash	10.18	11.07	13.01	14.83
Calcium	1.15	1.36	1.60	2.16
Phosphorus	0.29	0.36	0.38	0.41
Magnesium	0.42	0.45	0.48	0.52
Sodium	0.08	0.11	0.14	0.18
Chlorine	0.26	0.30	0.37	0.48

(David Mckenzie, *Goat Husbandry*, pp. 153, 157.)

Browse from Hedgerows

Hedgerows are a form of fence, and they are best used as such. Aside from their nutritional aspects, they provide shelter from the wind for your stock and wildings. They are also a year-long entrancement of plants, birds, insects, reptiles and mammals which helps increase the diversity of your local ecosystem. If you have no room for a woodlot, hedges can also be planted with fuel species for coppicing and can serve as an auxiliary herb garden for some of the wilder species of medicinal plants.

Like everything else, hedgerows require some planning, labor, and money to establish and maintain. Depending upon the variety of plants used, their size, soil fertility and moisture, they may take from four to eight years to become significant. Competition from existing weeds such as thistles, quackgrass, the bunch grasses, and blackberries will be serious unless measures are taken to deal with them.

Whether your planting will be piecemeal or all at once, soil preparation is best begun in the previous year. Spring tilling and summer harrowing will kill most of the quackgrass and thistles. A late summer sowing of an overwintering green manure crop will improve the soil fertility. This can be turned-in in the spring and a short ground cover grass such as a creeping red fescue can be sown along with any available flower seeds. Creeping red fescue, (or one of the dwarf ryes[1]), is short enough to need mowing only around the hedge plants when they are young, and it will prevent entrance of most annual weeds. A quick check several times a summer will serve to eliminate those few that do enter the row. When you wish to prepare a spot for new hedgerow plants you can put down a mulch of black plastic, cardboard, straw, or sawdust to kill the grass.

Stock hedge plants should be placed so that they are protected from animals when small, but close enough to grow through a fence so that they can be eaten as desired. The animals will keep them pruned on their side, but you will have to take care of the rest. This is best done when the stock will benefit from the extra rations, and will of course make the hedge denser.[2]

I list below a few shrub and tree species, both native and imported, that are most useful in the edible winter hedge. The starred ones are recommended by McKenzie as especially good for cool seasons. You can refer to Levy for medicinal herbs, and to Stanford[3] for fuel plants. For native shrubs, Joy Spurr's *Wild Shrubs, Finding and Growing Your Own,* is helpful, and Art Kruckeberg's *Gardening with Native Plants of the Pacific Northwest* is excellent.

If you are short on cash, read up on plant propagation (see References). As you drive around keep your eye out for suitable shrubbery. Most people who have a nice plant are happy to share a few clippings. Some of the best winter plants can also be started from seed.

Hedge Plants for the Maritime Northwest

This list omits many plant varieties good for summer use. Asterisk * indicates best midwinter plants.

APPLE/CRABAPPLE *Malus spp.* The fruits are very good for stock in the fall. Twigs in winter, prunings in spring.

ASH* *Fraxinus spp.* There is a native Oregon Ash which is rare in Washington but seems to grow in every swale of the

Willamette Valley. If you live up north and have trouble finding seedlings, you can buy one of the Eastern or European species from a nursery.

BEECH *Fagus spp.* The nuts are a traditional fall stock fattener.

BIRCH *Betula occidentalis.* Native hedge plant in eastern Washington. Good for spring and fall.

BLACKTHORN *Prunus spinosa.* European. Buy from a nursery or get cuttings from friends.

BLUEBERRY *Vaccinium spp.* If you have your own blueberry plants maybe you can propagate a few for the hedge. Wild blueberries are good; they can be found in the Cascade foothills.

BRAMBLES *Rubus spp.* Raspberries and blackberries. If you do plant these, remember that they spread like mad and have to be controlled. At least get good fruiting varieties; thornless blackberries would be good. Use starts from your own plants if you have them. Good for winter and early spring.

CHESTNUT *Castanea spp.* Nuts are used to fatten stock (especially pigs) in fall.

ELDER *Sambucus nigra.* Native east of the Cascades. Get seed, or try root divisions or seedlings.

ELM* *Ulmus spp.* Easy and vigorous

HAWTHORN *Crataegus monogyna, C. oxycanthus.* These are the European native species. Don't get the cultivars with double flowers as they don't set fruit. You can occasionally find native Black fruited hawthorn *(C. douglasii)* by roadsides, etc.

HAZEL *Corylus cornuta.* A native that can be found everywhere. Highly nutritious; good in early spring, February/ March. A relative of filberts *(C. avellana)* which are easy from seed. Easy and vigorous.

HEATHER* *Erica spp.* English, but horticultural varieties available from nurseries. Excellent from autumn to midwinter. Difficult, needs special growing conditions.

HOLLY* *Ilex aquifolium.* European. Common here as both an ornamental and a commercial crop. Goats devour it with glee all winter (and summer, too!). Easy and vigorous.

HONEYSUCKLE *Lonicera periclymenum caprifolium.* Introduced. Good goat fare; makes hedge denser by twining through it. This is the common sweet smelling honeysuckle so often planted. Cuttings are easy. Goats *might* also like the orange flavored native, *L. ciliosa.*

HUCKLEBERRY *Vaccinium ovatum.* Common Evergreen Huckleberry. Bears dark blue berries till late December. Common on Vashon Island in deep woods. Red Huckleberry, *V. parvifolium,* is common in the foothills growing from old cedar stumps. Sheep like the leaves.

IVY* *Hedera helix.* Imported; common and easy to start, but hard to get rid of! Good all winter.

MAPLE *Acer spp.* Pigs and cows appreciate the sweet leaves in the fall. Cows and goats will eat the bark and twigs all year.

MOUNTAIN ASH *Sorbus spp.* Sheep like the leaves; ducks, chickens, and wild birds like the berries.

WILLOW* *Salix spp.* Provides good winter feed for cows, sheep, and goats. The earliest blooming willows give bee forage in February.

1. The best short grass mixture I know of so far is called Companion and is a mixture of 80% Elka, a slow growing turf type perennial ryegrass, and 20% Ensylva, a creeping red fescue. It was developed for orchards and is available from Hobbs and Hopkins Ltd., 3964 S.E. Ankeny, Portland, OR 97214. (503) 239-7518. Another alternative is 100% Kentucky Blue Grass. This would be good to mix with herb plants, as it's not so aggressive in its growth.
2. Methods for trimming (or laying, as it is called in England) hedges are to be found in *The Complete Book of Self Sufficiency* by J. Seymour, or *Hedgerow* by Thomas and White.
3. See page 84, *The Next Whole Earth Catalog.*

Winter Crops for Livestock References
Common Herbs for Natural Health. Juliet de Bairacli Levy. 1974. Schocken Books, New York.
   Once you have the trees, shrubs and vines of your hedgerow planted you might want to use this book for ground cover suggestions.

Fertility Pastures. Newman Turner. 1975. Rateaver, Pauma Valley, CA 92061.
   This reprint of the 1955 Faber and Faber classic is one of the books you can read to learn about increasing and maintaining fertility by the use of green manures and special pasture mixes for leys (temporary pastures) that serve as part of the large scale rotation of crops on farms. Emphasizes various grasses and herbs. Focused on cows.

The Future is Abundant: A Guide to Sustainable Agriculture. 1982. L. Korn, B. Snyder, and M. Musick, editors. Tilth Associastion.
   Lots of information about regional horticulture. A plant species index to help you determine where to place plants in the environment.

Goat Husbandry. David McKenzie. 1956. Faber & Faber, 3 Queen Square, London WC1, England.
   Another of Faber's classic agriculture books. Fantastic scope and detail, worth it even if you don't have goats. Pertinent to the care of any grazing animal.

Gardening with Native Plants of the Pacific Northwest: an Illustrated Guide. Arthur R. Kruckeberg. 1982. University of Washington Press, Seattle and London.
   Well worth buying and treasuring. Covers propagation by a botany professor at the University of Washington who helped start the Washington Native Plant Society. For information on local chapters write to Betty Jo Fitzgerald, Secretary, WNPS, P.O. Box 1666, Olympia, WA 98507, or phone (206) 866-5607. Dr. Kruckeberg's wife, Mareen, runs MS.K., a small nursery which carries some native plants.

Hedgerow. Eric Thomas and John T. White. 1980. William Morrow & Co., New York.
   Very pretty book and a good, though short, introduction to the history, botany, wildlife, and folk uses of hedgrows in England.

Hedges. E. Pollard, M. D. Hooper, and N. W. Moore. 1975. Taplinger Publishing Co., New York.

Comprehensive work on nature and effect of hedges on landscape and farming. History, Flora, Fauna, Farmers Hedge.

Herbal Handbook for Farm and Stable. Juliette de Bairacli Levy. 1952. Faber & Faber, 99 Main Street, Salem, NH 03079.

A Rodale Press paperback reprint is available. An invaluable aid to weaning yourself and your stock from standard allopathic Western medicine.

Plants and Beekeeping. F. N. Howes. 1979. Faber & Faber, 29 Thompson Rd., Winchester, MA 01890 (617) 721-1427.

Read this to know what to plant to make your hedges and garden a bee's paradise. A new edition of the 1945 classic.

Plant Propagation. Philip McMillan Browse. 1979. Simon and Schuster, New York (in cooperation with the Royal Horticultural Society).

One of the easiest books on plant propagation with step-by-step illustrations of propagation methods. An excellent book from a good series on gardening. Available from Smith and Hawken (see Suppliers).

Plant Propagation: Principles and Practices. 3rd ed. 1975. H. T. Hartman and D. E. Kester. U.C. Davis.

The most complete book on plant propagation.

Trees and Bushes of Europe. Oleg Polunin. 1976. Oxford University Press, London, New York, Toronto.

A goody for naturalists and those who wish to understand the natural habitat of introduced European plants.

Wild Shrubs, Finding and Growing Your Own. Joy Spur. 1978. Pacific Search Press.

Very helpful for native shrubs.

Northwoods Nursery, 28696 S. Cramer Rd., Molalla, OR 97038.

"Trees for food, wildlife, woodlots and beauty." Try them for hedgerow plants.

Seed Companies

Nowadays I mostly order from two or three companies. It simplifies my life. But when you are starting out reading many seed catalogs is almost as educational as reading many gardening books. And for the rare variety or plant you often have to search about a bit. Have fun!

ABUNDANT LIFE SEED FOUNDATION, P. O. Box 722, Port Townsend, WA 98368.

Catalog and newsletter, $3.00 a year. Untreated seeds, no hybrids. Many seeds locally grown. Good folks.

JOHN BARBER LTD., 2 St. Andrew St., Hertford SG14 1JD, England.

A small company that does not regularly ship overseas. They will send an odd packet if you can't get a variety elsewhere.

CHASE COMPOST SEEDS LTD., Benhall, Saxmundham, Suffolk, England.

Organically grown seeds; winter hardy varieties and some unusual ones for the rest of the year. Recommended by some International Federation of Organic Agricultural Movements members. They have pasture herbs in agricultural quantities.

ELYSIAN HILLS, Bill and Mary Lou Schmidt, RFD #1, Box 200, Brattleboro, VT 05301.

Gillfeather turnip only. See *Horticulture* Magazine, November 1981.

HASTINGS: SEEDSMEN TO THE SOUTH, 434 Marietta St. NW, P.O. Box 4274, Atlanta, GA 30302.

Strongly oriented to the home gardener; lots of suggestions for early spring and late fall gardens for the Southeast.

J.A. DEMONCHAUX CO., 827 N. Kansas Ave., Topeka, KS 66608.

U.S. outlet for the French company Vilmorin-Andrieux. Small listing with some winter types.

JOHNNY'S SELECTED SEEDS, Albion, ME 04910.

Untreated seeds, many grown organically on their farm.

Specializes in short season varieties, some from Europe. Probably the most intelligent and reliable of the newer northern seed companies. Lots of cultural information. One of my favorites for summer varieties too.

KITAZAWA, 356 West Taylor St., San Jose, CA 95111.
  Japanese varieties.

NICHOLS GARDEN NURSERY; HERB AND RARE SEEDS, 1190 North Pacific Hwy., Albany, OR 97321.
  Now carrying more maritime-oriented seeds. Still doesn't make full use of the great range of European-bred seeds.

PARK SEED CO., INC., P.O. Box 31, Greenwood, SC 29646.
  Mostly flowers but many interesting ones that northern East Coast companies don't carry because they won't overwinter in continental climates. *Some* vegetables of use to winter cropping.

THE REDWOOD CITY SEED COMPANY, P.O. Box 361, Redwood City, CA 94064.
  Some interesting and unusual vegetables and herbs. Recommended by California gardeners.

RICHTERS, Goodwood, Ontario, Canada L0C 1A0. Catalog $1.00.
  The mecca for unusual herb seed. If you can't find it anywhere else, try here.

SEED SAVERS' EXCHANGE, c/o Whealy, Rt. 2, Princeton, MO 64673.
  A seed sharing group. Membership $6.00 a year; some maritime Northwest members. Well worth joining for the information alone, but the varieties available are amazing and usually found nowhere else. Harvest edition reports on conferences, seed saving tips, and other fascinating details.

SHELLEY AND STEPH SEEDS, 46525 McKensie Hwy., Vida, OR 97488.
  New, small offering, organically grown.

STOKES SEED, Box 548, Buffalo, NY 14240.
  Established quality company; wide selection home and com-

mercial; comprehensive seed starting directions. Some treated.

SUTTONS SEEDS LTD., Hele Rd., Torquay, Devon, TQ2 7QJ England.

The Stokes of England. Many interesting hardy varieties. Catalog $.50. *In spite of airmail and exchange rates* you get your money's worth of seed.

TANSY HERB FARM, 5888 Else Rd., Agassiz, B.C. V0M 1A0.

Run by Karen and John Balf. They sell plants in the Granville Market in Vancouver; these can be taken over the U.S. border as houseplants. They also do some mail order of seed.

TAYLORS HERB GARDENS, 1535 Lone Oak Rd., Vista, CA 92083.

Live plants only.

TERRITORIAL SEED CO., P.O. Box 27, Lorane, OR 97541.

"Garden seed for growing west of the Cascades." Started in 1980, Territorial is working assertively at collecting maritime adapted varieties (winter and summer) and running trials on them in Lorane.

TILLINGHAST SEED COMPANY, P.O. Box 738, LaConner, WA 98257.

Tillinghast has been serving the Northwest since 1885. It was bought by Arberta Lammers and Brian Scheuch in 1981 and they are beginning to carry more locally adapted modern varieties.

TSANG AND MA INTERNATIONAL, Box 294, Belmont, CA 94002.

Chinese varieties. A few Asian brassicas useful for spring/fall harvests and cloche/coldframe planting.

WELLSWEEP HERB FARM, 317 Mt. Bethel Rd., Port Murray, NJ 07865. Catalog $.75.

Live plants and dried flowers. Good for those herbs that cannot be reliably started from seed.

WILLIAM DAM SEEDS LTD., P.O. Box 8400, Dundas, Ontario, Canada L9H 6M1.

Some good fall and winter varieties. Stock kales. Untreated.

Books You Should Read and General References

The Beautiful Food Garden, Kate Rogers Gessert, 1983, Van Nostrand Reinhold Company, New York.

If you need help designing your garden for attractiveness as well as nutrition and ease of cultivation you might check this out of the library. Ms. Gessert resides in Portland, Oregon.

Better Vegetable Gardens the Chinese Way. Peter Chan and Spencer Gill. 1977. Graphic Arts Center, 2000 N.W. Wilson, Portland, OR 97209.

The authors have a wry sense of humor that appeals to me, and the photographs show another culture's version of raised permanent beds. You can probably find it in a library. Some winter cropping information.

Colour in the Winter Garden. Graham Stuart Thomas. 1967. Phoenix House, London; and Charles T. Branford Co., Newton Center, MA.

This is about ornamentals, but once you achieve year-round vegetable gardening consciousness you might want to extend your joy in this direction. One of my very favorite books.

The Complete Guide to Organic Gardening West of the Cascades. Steve Solomon. 1981. Pacific Search Press, Seattle.

Steve Solomon moved to Oregon in 1979 and now runs Territorial Seed Co. Not "complete," but interesting reading nonetheless. Some of the statements in the first seventy pages are outrageous and hasty. A few serious omissions (like no mention of Tilth Association). The bulk of the book, on the vegetable families, is better and shows thought and good research.

The Complete Vegetable Grower. W. E. Shewell-Cooper. 1975. Faber & Faber, 39 Thompson Rd., Winchester, MA 01890.

I like this book even better than when I read it the first time in 1975. That is to say, I've experimented and learned a lot since then, and now I can appreciate it more. It is written by a professional English horticulturalist. One of the better modern sources for maritime gardeners.

Growing Vegetables in the Pacific Northwest. Cecil Solly. 1938-1951.

A classic from the Forties, now out of print and available only in libraries.

Grow Your Own Fruits and Vegetables. L. D. Hills. 1975. Faber and Faber, 39 Thompson Rd., Winchester, MA 01890.

For more experienced gardeners. Half of the book is devoted to the organic culture of vegetables in a maritime climate. Hills is the director of the Henry Doubleday Research Association (see Organizations)..

Know and Grow Vegetables (1979) and *Know and Grow Vegetables 2* (1982). J. K. A. Bleasdale, D. J. Slater et al. Oxford University Press, London, New York, Toronto.

Two fascinating volumes jam-packed with basic information, all supported by years of careful research at the National Vegetable Research Station, Warwickshire, England. Very useful for maritime gardeners. Order from Oxford University Press, 16-00 Pollip Dr., Fairlawn, NJ 07410.

The New Vegetable Grower's Handbook. A. J. Simons. 1975 edition. Penguin Books Canada Ltd., 2801 John St., Markham, Ontario, Canada L3R 1B4.

An encyclopedia-type listing of vegetable crops and when to grow them. Quite useful but hard to get.

Organic Gardening. Lawrence D. Hills. 1981. Penguin Books.

A very good basic book for those wishing to understand and practice organic vegetable production in a northern maritime climate. Hills has over forty years of horticultural experience and it comes across on every page. Very useable in the maritime Northwest as crops, pests, and diseases are so similar, or identical to those of Britain. Available from Richters.

Salads the Year Round. Joy Larkcom. 1980. Hamlyn Publishing Group Ltd.

Available from the Tilth Association, Seattle Chapter (see organizations). A very good book by a happy vegetable fanatic. Full of good information. If you like salads you shouldn't be without it.

The Self-sufficient Gardener. John Seymour. 1979. Doubleday, New York.

One of the best of John Seymour's many good books. Though vegetable growing directions are a bit scanty, the overall scope is excellent for those who like the visual approach. Includes fruits.

The Simon and Schuster Step by Step Encyclopedia of Practical Gardening: Vegetables. Tony Biggs. 1980. Simon and Schuster, New York.

This book is neither fish nor fowl, neither truly British (maritime) nor American (continental). Hence, it ends up as a bunch of pictures of use only to the beginning gardener. The least useful (so far) of a good series.

ORGANIZATIONS

CITY FARMER. Suite 801, 318 Haner Street, Vancouver, B.C. V6B 2V3.

Focusing on urban agriculture and the politics of food gardening. Sponsors education courses, newsletter, etc.

ECOLOGY ACTION OF THE MIDPENINSULA, 2225 El Camino Real, Palo Alto, CA 94306.

Publishers of John Jeavon's book. Puts out a "Self-Teaching Mini Series" and various other materials. Largely oriented to warm areas (in other words, California).

HENRY DOUBLEDAY RESEARCH ASSOCIATION, Convent Lane, Bocking, Braintree, Essex, England.

$10 a year for membership. Book and rare seed source.

INTEGRAL URBAN HOUSE AND FARALLONES INSTITUTE, 1516 5th Street, Berkeley, CA 94710.

Intelligent information on ecological living, from solar energy food production to waste recycling.

INTERNATIONAL FEDERATION OF ORGANIC AGRICULTURAL MOVEMENTS (IFOAM).

Most European countries have IFOAM members. You can get a list of IFOAM members from the Seattle Tilth office (see below).

SOLAR SURVIVAL, Harrisville, NH 03450.

Plans for solar pods, cones, etc.

TILTH ASSOCIATION, 4649 Sunnyside No., Seattle, WA 98103.

Tilth is a non-profit association in the Pacific Northwest which links urban and rural people devoted to a sustainable regional agriculture. Tilth members are active in growing food, saving farmland, developing local markets, improving forest practices and doing whatever they can to contribute to regional agriculture and forestry.

In the past eight years, Tilth has grown to a regional association with 1800 members and 15 chapters. Tilth chapter activities include social events, farm tours, work exchanges, research projects, demonstration gardens, conferences, and farmers' markets.

The Tilth Newsletter serves as a quarterly source of information and inspiration for people interested in environmentally sound approaches to farming and gardening in our region. Each issue is packed with practical, philosophical and political news as well as information for gardeners, homesteaders and farmers.

Membership in the Tilth Association, which includes a subscription to the quarterly journal, is $10 per year.

Since Tilth is a regional association made up of local groups working to create a new agriculture for the Pacific Northwest, the best way to get personally involved is through one of the local chapters. If you are interested, contact one of the people listed below. Many of the chapters have their own newsletters, and sponsor workshops and other exciting projects.

South Humboldt
  Ram Fishman
  3010 Ettersburg Rd.
  Garberville, CA 95440
  (707) 986-7504
Siskiyou
  Tom Ward
  100 Eagle Mill Rd.
  Ashland, OR 97520
  (503) 482-0320 (Tzac Owens)
Rogue
  Jody Weiner
  348 Hussey Lane
  Grants Pass, OR 97526
  (503) 476-8979
Willamette Valley
  Tom Forster
  3586 Willamette
  Eugene, OR 97405
  (503) 345-1218

Southwest Washington
  Gary Kline
  820 No. Puget
  Olympia, WA 98506
  (206) 257-6236
Seattle
  Regina Hugo
  4649 Sunnyside No.
  Seattle, WA 98103
  (206) 633-0451
Nooksack
  Gretchen Hoyt
  3550 Alm Rd.
  Everson, WA 98247
  (206) 966-4157
Good Earth
  Scott McManus
  Rt. 1, Box 372
  Cashmere, WA 98815
  (509) 782-3325

Okanogan
  Michael Pilarski
  P.o. Box 1050
  Tonasket, WA 98855
  (509) 485-3169
Northern Idaho
  Stephen Bishop
  P.O. Box 509
  Sagle, ID 83860
  (208) 263-8627
Santa
  Janice Masterjohn
  Rt. 4, Box 152
  St. Maries, ID 83861
  (208) 245-3685

Spokane
  Tom Tuffin
  No. 225 Division St. #30
  Spokane, WA 99202
  (509) 236-2353
South Whidbey
  Marianne Edain
  Box 53
  Langley, WA 98260
  (206) 221-2332
Methow
  Bob Elk
  P.O. Box 512
  Methow, WA 98834
  (509) 923-2411
Palouse
  Nathan Jacobsen
  S.E. 320 High St.
  Pullman, WA 99163

SUPPLIERS

GRO-TEK, Home Greenhouse Supplies and Services, RFD #1, Box 518A, South Berwick, ME 03908.

HORTICULTURAL TOOL AND SUPPLY CATALOG, A. M. Leonard, 6665 Spiker Road, Piqua, OH 45356.

INDOOR GARDEN SUPPLY INC., P.O. Box 17011, Seattle, WA 98107.
  Source of Safer's Insecticidal Soap.

PICKEN & SON LTD., Frankfort St., Works, Birmingham, B19 2YL, England.
  The only source I know for the original Chase cloche wires.

SMITH AND HAWKINS TOOL COMPANY, 68 Homer Street, Palo Alto, CA 94301.
  Excellent garden tools; books from England and elsewhere.

WALT NICKE, Box 667g, Hudson, NY 12534.
  More garden tools.
Also check in the Whole Earth Catalogs.